Into the Heat

Fighting Fires in Baltimore City

Other Books by 1st Ride Publishing:

Science Fiction / Adventure

The Champion of Clarendon Ditch Trilogy by Matt Galeone

The Champion of Clarendon Ditch: Book 1 –The Hatching (2012)

The Champion of Clarendon Ditch: Book 2 –The Alliance (2012)

The Champion of Clarendon Ditch: Book 3 –The Champion (2012)

The 15th Chair Trilogy by Matt Galeone

The 15th Chair: Book 1 - The Journey (2014)

The 15th Chair: Book 2 - The Return (coming 2016)

Dramatic Fiction

An Image of Us, Robert G. Edwards (2013)

Purple Meadow, Robert G. Edwards (2013)

Chasing the Surface, Robert G. Edwards (2014)

The Amalgamist, Cristel Orrand (2014)

Khayal, Cristel Orrand (2015)

Horror

Withered Hosts, Scott Bisig (2014)

Creative Non-Fiction

Getting Home, Kim Manuelides (2015)

Books by 1st Ride Kids

The Special Beat of Ordinary Feet, Patricia Perrin (2013)

Sparky & Squeaker, Jen Katz (2013)

Willoughby's Whiskers, Patricia Perrin (2015)

Helping Hooves & Humongous Hearts, Beth Williams (2015)

Oberst & Valentine Find Their Human, Matt Galeone (2015)

For a current listing of 1st Ride Publishing's library of published works check our website at:
http://1strideenterprises.com/books/

Into the Heat

Fighting Fires in Baltimore City

Ray Lockett

Edited by Beth Williams
Proofread by Amy Beth Leasure
Layout by Katherine Savery Gray

A Story from 1st Ride Publishing

1st Ride Publishing

This is a memoir and includes events, locations and conversations from the author's memory. Some names and identifying characteristics have been changed in order to maintain anonymity.

ISBN 978-1515285144

Dedication

I would like to dedicate this book to my Father-in-Law, the late James M. Gallagher, killed in the line of duty with the Baltimore City Fire Department on July 15, 1961.

Table of Contents

Acknowledgements

I would like to thank the following people. Jim Keefe for his relentless encouragement to get my book published. He rode with Truck 10 and Truck 13 with permission to take photographs. He graciously provided them for use in my book. My mother, the late Barbara Lockett, who kept scrapbooks for most of my career without which I could never have put a timeline together. Emergency Vehicle Driver Jim Vodarick from Truck 5 who asked me to allow his friend Matt Galeone, one of the Publishers from 1st Ride Enterprises, to read my book. Beth Williams, Publisher from 1st Ride Enterprises, for her guidance and knowledge as she took me step by step through the process that led to the finished product of Into The Heat. Both of my sons, Ray and Steve, for not only being excellent Firefighters but most importantly being wonderful sons and caring fathers. Finally, my wife Lois, without her computer skills, her encouragement, her patience and her ability to keep me focused, I would be lost.

Introduction

When my father came to me and told me he was in the process of writing a book, I could only think, "This should be interesting." I knew my Dad had spent most of his 29 years in service in some of the busiest firehouses in Baltimore. Also being a firefighter, I knew how our senses of humor and views of the world can be misconstrued by others as callous and even mean at times. As the process continued and I read excerpts of his transcript, I realized that my Dad's wonderful way of telling stories and his exuberant sense of humor came to life in his pages.

It brought back many memories of my childhood – a childhood that in many ways prepared my brother and me for the life of a fireman. The number one rule my father taught us is that family comes first. We all have each other's back. He also taught us that we are responsible for our own actions and that those actions have repercussions. I don't know if they were already instilled in him before he joined the Department, but these same morals are the backbone of being not only just a good firefighter but a good firefighting company.

I am not bragging when I say that by the time I entered the Department, my father had an excellent reputation throughout the Fire Department. As a kid, I always thought of him as a hero. Now that I'm grown up, in the Department, and a father myself, I've come to realize that he not only was a good firefighter but also a great father and man. My one thought after reading his book is that I hope my kids will one day look at me the way that I look at him.

I hope you enjoy reading this book and experiencing the ups and downs of a firefighter's life. It is a unique perspective into the physical and psychological journey of a firefighter and father. Through the eyes of one firefighter who worked in the most poverty stricken neighborhoods in Baltimore City, you will experience laughter, anger and tears. The life of a firefighter is a journey that can only be told and a lot of the times understood by firefighters. My father's way of telling the story of his career will give those who always wanted to know what we really do, a peek behind the curtain. I am proud to be his son, colleague and a friend. I don't think it is a coincidence that my brother and I followed in his footsteps. Now turn the page and embark on the adventure to see why family comes first.

Steve Lockett
BCFD

Ray Lockett at another burned-out crack house. (Unknown)

Part I

Breaking in the Rookie on the West Side

Ray Lockett, two years in the Fire Department. (Unknown)

CHAPTER 1
The Rookie

I'm sitting at the watch desk at 4 a.m., wide awake and nervous as a whore in church. The last thing the Lieutenant said to me was, "If they call one of these numbers on the desk, throw the gong." I'm studying the numbers like I'm going to memorize them in the next five minutes. Never mind that there are approximately 40 or so numbers, almost all starting with number 3. Some are two digits, some three or more. All of them are the numbers of the alarm boxes that Engine 25 takes on the first alarm. The other three men at work this night are all in bed upstairs. All are multi-year veterans and had no trouble falling asleep after our return from a signal 30 (false alarm) at 3 a.m.

The watch desk is silent for the first 25 minutes I'm on duty when suddenly the dispatcher says, "Alert, building fire, Fremont Ave. and Laurens St., box 373." Now I know that has to be on this desk somewhere, but I'm looking so fast that I can't find it. The dispatcher repeats it and now I'm starting to panic. I can hear the guys in the bunkroom pulling on their boots and sliding the brass pole to the apparatus floor. I still haven't found the damn number and the Lieutenant is now standing next to me. I look at him and in a voice at least two octaves too high I say, "I can't find the number!" He says, "It's us, just get on the pumper," in a voice that's as cool as can be. I get on and out we go onto McCullough St. We hang a left and another quick left onto Gold St. Three blocks later and it's another left on to Pennsylvania Ave. Its 4:30 in the morning but this is West Baltimore and there are people everywhere. We bear right at Fremont and we are suddenly in a fog bank. You can't see two feet in front of you. The oldest member of Engine 25 gets out and starts to walk in front of the pumper. It's the only way we can keep moving without hitting something. I suddenly realize we aren't in fog, we're in smoke and it's down to the street level. We go 100 yards and stop. "Right here," the Lieutenant says and we exit the pumper.

I look to my right and I see it, a large one story body and fender shop. Smoke is pouring out from all around the wide rolling door and the whole building is engulfed in smoke. We pull the inch and a half hose off and drag it to the door. Like most buildings in West Baltimore, this building is locked up like Fort Knox. There is no way in except to wait for the truck company to force a door. We stand there with a charged line and watch as the truck men start to cut a hole in the rolling door. It's a heavy metal door and progress is slow. Meanwhile, Battalion Chief 4 has asked for a second alarm and Rescue 1 shows up with large railroad jacks and proceeds to lift the door about three feet. "Here we go," the Lieutenant says and we start to crawl in. I have on ¾ boots but they might as well be 1/3 boots because I forget to pull the tops up. Turnout coat, gloves and a helmet make up the rest of my ensemble. No breathing apparatus back then, you were expected to take the smoke and heat until you were relieved by someone with a mask on. God I can't see anything, can't breathe, my nose is running and my lungs feel like someone lit a blow torch in there. My Lieutenant has his knee in my back and is pushing me forward, all the while telling me to stay down and keep moving. We crawl forward and I can see a glow to my left. "Hit it," he says and I point the nozzle in that direction and open it up. The smoke immediately gets worse and the Lieutenant pushes my face down next to the nozzle where the force from the water exiting the nozzle has created a small space of air. I take a small gulp of air and we start forward again. I can hear other hoses and men near us but visibility is zero. We get closer and I can see that besides the office that is burning, so are two or three cars. We are pouring water on them and they are darkening down. "It looks like we got the worst of it out," I hear someone say and we shut the hose down to take a look. My Lieutenant taps me on the shoulder and says to follow the line out and take a break. I turn and crawl out the way I came in. All this time my boots are filling up with water. I feel as if I'm going to throw up and that's just what I do as soon as I crawl under the rolling door and get to the fresh air. I'm at the feet of one of the Chiefs and he asks me if I am alright. I stand up and mutter that I'm fine and stagger away.

This was my first official night in the fire department and I had started it out with a bang. I had a headache for two days and coughed up black phlegm for another two days. But at the time I couldn't wait to get home and tell my wife about the fire, the guys I worked with, and the adrenalin rush I got going in there.

Growing up, I never had any intentions of becoming a firefighter. You know how some kids are always talking about the firemen or the fire trucks. That was not me. I didn't know any firefighters as a child so my main ambition was the same as most of the kids in Northeast Baltimore in the 50's and 60's. We all wanted to be cowboys. Gunsmoke was on, Rawhide was a big hit as were numerous other westerns. The only contact I had with the fire department was a single firehouse that sat on White Ave. This was the home of Engine 54 at the time and some of us from the neighborhood would go over there on Saturday and watch cartoons with the firefighters. I don't ever recall seeing them go out the door for any reason, which at the time was not unusual as they were one of the least busy companies in the city.

Growing up in our neighborhood was both good and bad. Our neighborhood consisted of three blocks of semi-detached houses with four families to a duplex. Five people lived in our apartment: my mother, two uncles, my grandmother and me. We lived in a one floor, two-bedroom apartment. My two uncles slept on a pull out bed in the living room, my grandmother had her own room and my mother and I slept in another small bedroom. My father had left before I was born, however this was not uncommon in our tight little group of friends. There were eight of us that hung together and only one had both a mother and a father. We were happy and didn't know any different. Days were spent playing baseball in the summer and football in the winter. This was not little league as is so common today. We would make our own field of dreams behind the apartments and play until dark. Over the years we all went our separate ways and only a few of us still keep in contact. I was the only one that became a firefighter. Some died of a drug overdose and one went to jail.

In April of 1964, I enlisted in the army at the age of seventeen to avoid what I thought was going to be a trip to the juvenile detention center or worse, I spent three years in the infantry which is where most high school dropouts ended up. Upon my release from Uncle Sam, I had to find work. I took a job placement test but there were no openings for a highly qualified machine gunner.

As I continued my quest for a job, I started dating the same girl I was dating before I joined the army. We had kept in touch while I was in the service and I couldn't wait to start up where we had left off. I found work on the Pennsylvania Railroad as a brakeman, but I didn't have a car and the job was in Washington DC. The grind of taking two buses, a train and two more buses to get to work quickly ended that plan. Even though I didn't have a decent job with a future, Lois and I got married on June 22, 1968. It must have been true love, because we have been married over forty years. She told me years before that her father (James Gallagher) had been killed in the line of duty with the

Baltimore City Fire Department in 1961. Later I would come to understand how traumatic that really was for her.

During those years, I was jumping from job to job. Some I was laid off from, some I was fired from and some I just quit. I never went long without a job but then again, I never stayed very long either. Over a four year span I must have had a dozen jobs, and now I had another mouth to feed. My son Ray was born on June 26, 1970. It was now 1972 and I was still trying to find something that was worthwhile to do for the rest of my life. My mother-in-law who I am sure was tired of seeing her only daughter married to a guy who had no direction in his life, mentioned that the fire department was giving their test in the near future. I decide to take it as did my brother-in-law, Jim.

We went together to what was then the Baltimore Civic Center. We parked and walked two blocks to the civic center, which was also home to a minor league hockey team. When we turned the corner, we stopped where we were. The line snaked around the building and out of sight. "There must be a mistake," I said, "the hockey team must be playing." We asked someone in line what they were there for. "The fire department test," he replied. "Come on, let's get out of here," I said to Jim, "I'm not waiting in this line." Patience was never my virtue but my brother-in-law had no qualms about waiting. We waited about half an hour and they let us in. The test was a civil service test, a lot of common sense questions, some math but nothing too hard. I was grateful for that. My education had come to a screeching halt half way through the tenth grade. My math teacher and I had a series of disagreements that led to expulsion. I was stupid for getting thrown out but I was smart enough to get my equivalency certificate in the army. We took the test and talked afterward about how we thought we had done. Jim thought he had done pretty well but I wasn't so sure about myself. I said, "there were an awful lot of guys there and I'm not the sharpest knife in the drawer." It took about a month to get the results and I opened the letter with trepidation. "Congratulations," it said. "You passed the test and you are number fifty two on the list." I was surprised and happy at the same time -- but I don't think I was as happy as my wife and her mother. I called Jim to see how he had done. I was a little hesitant to tell him about my score because he had a lot more schooling that I did. I didn't want to embarrass him. Yeah, fat chance. He had placed second but was having second thoughts about the fire department. In the end, I went into the fire academy and he changed his mind and went into another profession.

The fire academy was a one story large brick building on Pulaski Highway. It consisted of a handful of class rooms, a few offices and a large auditorium. Outside there were numerous buildings used to teach the basics of firefighting. A tower to rappel off of, a two story building to practice throwing ladders to and also to set fires in. There were two large diameter pits filled with a flammable liquid and a small metal hut that was called a Christmas tree. For the next eight weeks, we were to train here nine hours a day, five days a week. We were issued jump suits to wear and it felt like I was back in the army. However, the discipline part of it was nowhere near as strict as the army. Meeting the other men out there was an experience in itself. One guy asked me if I wanted to see a picture of his wife. "Sure," I said, "let me see it." He proceeded to show me a picture of his wife breast feeding his son. I told him I thought she had nice tits and he thanked me. I sat at another table after that. Thank God most of the guys in my class were not like that guy. I met one guy who never shut up. He talked about everything and anything but not like a know-it-all. He just liked to talk. Little did I know I would fight many a fire with him during my first eight years in the fire department. His name was Doug Falls, and we remain friends to this day.

Although I liked most of my time in fire school, I was glad when the powers-that-be changed our schedule. Now we had to report to fire school only three days a week. Twice a week we rode as the third man on an ambulance. On Saturdays we rode on one of the trucks or engines for the full day. It didn't take me long riding the ambulance to realize it was not my favorite thing to do. I was assigned to Ambulance 7. Our days were mostly filled with picking up drunks and drug addicts along Pratt Street. This was before the revitalization of the inner harbor, and it was not a pretty sight down there. You talk about a thankless job! In my opinion, it remains that way to this day. When you did get a run for a shooting, stabbing, or any other incident that was life or death, it was a very rewarding feeling to know you had saved someone's life.

The only trouble was that the bad runs far and away outnumbered the life or death runs. I did have one life or death run that bothered me more than I wanted to let on. A young girl was in juvenile court on the fifth floor. She was seated next to her mother when she got up, walked to the window and threw herself through the window to the alley below. When we pulled up, she was lying face down in the alley. She looked to be about 14 years old with long blonde hair. In those days there was no advanced medical care by the ambulance personnel. It was called swoop and scoop and that's what we did. It was obvious from her massive head injuries that she was beyond help. We rushed to Mercy Hospital, just a few short blocks away. We took her into the emergency room where the doctors and nurses rushed her into the back room. We went with them and I watched as they did what they could, but it was too late. I went back out to the waiting room to collect my thoughts and the girl's mother came rushing in. Seeing my uniform she knew I must have brought her daughter in. The look on her face was almost more than I could bear. "How is she," she asked me, "is she going to make it?" I could only tell her that the doctors were working on her and they would let her know. It was our last run of the day and when I got home I could not stop thinking about it. I sat down with my wife and told her about it. It was my first experience of that kind and it really shook me up.

On Saturdays we rode with a company, either an engine or a truck. To the uninitiated, the engine carries the hose and the men go right to the seat of the fire to knock it down as quickly as possible. The truck, or ladder company as it is known in some cities, carries all the tools needed to force entry and to ventilate the building. It also carries different sized ladders for rescue. The job of the truck men is to ventilate the building and perform search and rescue. The company I rode with was Truck 4 in West Baltimore. They were stationed with Engine 13, Ambulance 4 and Battalion Chief 4 on the corner of McCullough Street and McMechen Street. This was a busy company and the men let us know that right away. There was the usual ridicule and good natured harassment and I could tell they really hoped we would get a fire while the new guy was there. I was told by the officer that if we did get "a shitter," to stick like glue to the oldest member of the company, a twenty year veteran who looked like he could holler at a fire and it would go out.

That afternoon we went out for a report of an apartment fire on the fourth floor at 900 Argyle Avenue. This building was part of the Murphy homes complex, comprised of four public housing buildings. It was one of the filthiest; most crime ridden high rises in the city. When we pulled up you could see the smoke curling out from the fourth floor window. I jumped off the truck and my mind was racing a mile a minute. I was trying to remember how to get the air mask out of the box and the proper way to put one on, when the old veteran grabbed me and said, "come on, we don't need a damn mask." Off we went to the stairs and up to the fourth floor. We got to the door leading to the long hallway and he said "put your hand on my belt and keep it there." I did like I was told and we entered the hallway. The smoke at our end of the hall was not too bad as we started down but the further we went, the lower the smoke got. I kept my hand on his belt but I didn't realize that he was stooping down lower and lower while I was walking upright. I was coughing and gagging as we got near the apartment. A lot of things were happening that I had no idea of; the hose had been stretched from the stand pipe and charged and the door was being forced open. I couldn't see any of this because my eyes were watering so badly from the smoke. When the engine men made their way in, we went right with them. I still had a death grip on my man's belt and he took me right through a smoke-filled room to a door that led to the balcony, and pushed me out the door on to the balcony. "Stay there," he said and disappeared back into the smoke. I stayed. After a few minutes he came back and got me. "It wasn't much," he said, "just a mattress and box spring in the bedroom." I helped with the overhaul, throwing the burned mattress and box spring out the window and cleaning up. As we rode back to the station I was thinking - I wonder if I will ever be able to do this job like these guys did theirs.

As my days wound down at fire school I looked forward to my new assignment, wherever that might be. I was worried that I might wind up going to a slow company, something I definitely didn't want to do. I really didn't want to take any chances that that would happen, so I decided to ask for a little help. At the time, I was playing fast pitch softball with a member of the fire department. His name was Tim Farner and he was our pitcher and was also active in the union. He later became union president and I still see him at union meetings. I asked him if there was anything he could do to get me in a busy company. He said he would do his best and he was true to his word. When the assignments came out I was assigned to Engine 25 at McCullough and Gold Streets. Only about five blocks from Truck 4, my Saturday company in fire school. I couldn't wait to start.

CHAPTER 2
First Assignment

Engine 25 was a big old firehouse, built in the early 1900's when the city was still using horses. It was two stories high and almost two hundred feet deep. The apparatus floor was cobblestone with a spiral staircase in the back. The spiral staircase was put in when the house was built to keep the horses from walking upstairs. The upstairs was the bunk room and the office. There were four holes in the floor with the brass poles to use for a speedy descent to the first floor. The kitchen and the watch desk were on the first floor. The hose tower was in the rear of the house and raised another story above the second floor. This was used to hang and dry the fifty foot sections of hose once a week to prevent mildew. I walked in carrying my gear thinking all I want to do is learn what to do and when to do it. One of the last things one of our instructors at fire school had told us was, "No matter what you learned here, your real learning doesn't start until you get in your company." How right he was.

I was starting on night work -- fourteen hours a night for four nights. My first four nights we had three working fires [what the firefighters called "good fires"] and too many other runs to count. Each morning I would stagger home, sleep until it was time to get up and go back to work. I had not yet mastered the art of sleeping in the firehouse. The watch desk would give out every run for every company in the city. This was easily heard upstairs and when we did get a few hours without a run, I would just lay there wide awake listening to the joker chop off boxes. The joker was a roll of ticker tape attached to a spool on top of the watch desk. When a box number was transmitted from communications, the corresponding numbers would be punched out on the tape. If it started out with the number three there was a very good chance we were going. It amazed me that the other guys in the house could sleep through that racket but when communications said one of our box numbers, they would wake up before the man on watch could throw the gong. I couldn't wait to get to where I could do that too.

After my two days off, which I really needed, it was back to work for my four days of day work. Day work was much different than night work. Fewer runs, fewer fires, a different routine altogether. First there was house work to do. Depending on what day of the week it was, we cleaned windows, shined poles, scrubbed floors, etc. I was learning all the mundane things that the public doesn't see. I was also getting to know the guys I would be working with. My Lieutenant was a big guy with a boisterous sense of humor, who had the respect of everyone we met. There were seven of us on C-shift but only four worked at the firehouse at a time. The other three guys were either on vacation or would be sent to another firehouse to fill a vacancy. As I was the new guy, I would work at Engine 25 for the first month before I would take my turn in the rotation of details to other houses. At Engine 25 there were four men who didn't take details, the Lieutenant, the pump operator (driver), the first acting Lieutenant and the first fill-in driver.

The first acting man, who takes over when the Lieutenant is off, was a 30 year veteran who seemed to be pretty much a grouch. That was my first impression and it turned out to be true. The pump operator was an Irishman named Brennan, straight from the old country. He still had the Irish brogue and was hard for me to understand but he was helpful around the firehouse. My favorite guy was a black guy who had about 15 years in the department. His name was James Schuster and he had a great sense of humor. We used to stay up late just talking about the right and the wrong way to do things. He talked about when he first joined the fire department and what it was like to be one of the first blacks. He didn't talk about it with any bitterness, just in an informative way. But I could tell the hurt was still there. He was a very good firefighter and he taught me a lot. Another member of Engine 25, Jim Sanders, had two more years than I did, which does not seem like much. But two years at Engine 25 was a lot more experience than two years at a slow house and he was also helpful. The last remaining member was a new guy like me. We had gone through fire school together and I knew him pretty well. We wouldn't get to work at Engine 25 together very much because they didn't want two new guys working at the same time. Jacob Clark was a very quiet guy who had spent a number of years in the navy on a submarine. With both of us being new, we had something in common right away and he had a great outlook on everything. Where I would get upset he would always find the funny side of things and the next thing I knew I'd be laughing. So that was our crew at Engine 25 and I don't think I could have started out my career in a better place.

Each day was a learning experience, but it was enjoyable. I looked forward to going to work. You never knew what you were going to run into. Early in June we were dispatched to the scene of a car wreck in Druid Hill Park. Upon our arrival, we saw that the car was upside down and a crowd had already gathered. We pulled one of the occupants out and he was screaming about his leg. We looked down and the lower part of his leg was missing. I was the rookie so naturally it was my job to crawl into the car and retrieve the rest of his leg. I got on my stomach, crawled in and spotted it right away. The shoe was still on the foot and I gingerly slid it toward me. It was then that I realized that it was an artificial leg so I had no reservations about picking it up. However, when I slid out of the car and stood up with the leg in my hand to announce that it was artificial the crowd started screaming and backing up. "No, no," I said, "It's okay, I've got it." It took awhile for the crowd to calm down and realize what was going on. The more we talked about it back at the firehouse the more we laughed. Firehouse humor can sometimes be described as sick but it is also a great way to cope with some of the things you see that the average person never experiences.

When I first got to Engine 25 they had just gotten a new pumper and you rode inside. When I got detailed to other companies, I rode the back step. I always liked riding the step until my first winter. Sometimes it got so cold, your fingers would not uncurl right away and you couldn't look where you were going because you could not breathe the cold air. It actually hurt your lungs. At that time, I was going through the process of getting approved to fill in as the pump operator. The new pumper was easy, but I also had to learn the old pumper because when our pumper broke we would be given one of the old ones. Those had no power steering and you had to double clutch to change gears. Driving was no problem. I had driven everything in the army from a jeep to a 5 ton truck to a 13 ton personnel carrier. I always liked to drive but it didn't take me long to realize that once you got there and got water, all the excitement was over. But for the man on the pipe, it was just beginning. I got a lot of time riding the pipe because the first acting man didn't want to do it anymore and that was fine with me.

I was also learning that there was a real rivalry between the companies. At this time, fire-alarm boxes were on street corners where anyone could pull them. The last thing you wanted was to be beaten in to your first-alarm box by other companies responding that were a little farther away. We would gloat if we beat Engine 13 or Engine 8 in to their first-alarm boxes. And if we got beat in on ours, we had to listen to them ask us if we came on the second alarm or if our firehouse doors were stuck down and we couldn't get out. None of this was done in a mean way but in a competitive way. I always thought that fighting fires was as close to playing big league sports as I was going to get. I know that sounds funny, after all it was life or death sometimes, but that's the way I felt.

Not long after I joined the department, I went to a bachelor party for an old friend. A bunch of us were winding the night down at a local bar when a fight broke out. I got sucker punched with a longneck beer bottle which broke my nose and opened a cut over my eye. When the fight was over, which took awhile as I was determined to get the guy that hit me, we went out to our cars and could see the police lights flashing and hear the sirens coming. It was almost 2 a.m. and I decided to go right to the firehouse because I had day work the next day anyway. I was quite a sight when I walked in. My nose was swollen, my shirt was ripped to shreds and there was blood all over me. I told the man on watch to mark me in for 6 a.m. and went up to bed, but when I laid down my nose was throbbing so bad I couldn't sleep. I got back up and went to the hospital where they confirmed that my nose was broken but the break was high up on the bridge and there was nothing they could do about it. They placed me off duty and sent me home. I had called my wife earlier to let her know I was going into work but I didn't tell her I had been in fight. I called her again, told her I was messed up and I was coming home. By now both my eyes were black and I didn't look too good. "What the hell" I thought, at least I'll get some sympathy at home. I walked in the kitchen door; my wife took one look at me and burst out laughing. "You look like a raccoon," she said. So much for sympathy!

A few days later I had to go in to work to fill out the paper work explaining how I was injured. James Schuster was in charge and had to take my statement. I couldn't tell him what really happened so I said a kid had run out in front of me on the way to work and I had to slam on my brakes. When I did, my hands slipped and I fell forward hitting my nose on the steering wheel. James looked at me, smiled, and said, "I'll write that down but what I want to know is why you just kept banging it on the wheel over and over!" We had a good laugh about that for a long time. I healed and nothing further was said about it, but I was a little more careful in bars after that.

Truck 10 in 1972; I was detailed there occasionally. (Unknown)

CHAPTER 3
Details and Medic Runs

When I was detailed to other companies, it was always in my own battalion, which was the fourth battalion. Our battalion consisted of Engine 25, Engine 7, Engine 52, Engine 13 and Engine 8. Also in the fourth battalion were Truck 4, Truck 10 and Ambulances 4 and 15. Engine 13, Truck 4, Ambulance 4 and Battalion Chief 4 were all in one house. The same was true of Engine 8, Truck 10 and Ambulance 15. The rest of the companies were all single houses. The worst thing about being detailed somewhere else was that somehow it was always your turn to ride the ambulance, which we also referred to as "ambo" or "medic." I didn't think I was going to like riding the ambo from my experience in fire school and I was right. You received your runs by telephone from communications, so when the phone rang you would just get up and start toward the unit. The phone rang all day and night without a letup, most of the time you would not make it back to the firehouse before you would get another run by radio. If these runs were all legitimate runs, i.e. shootings or stabbings, it would not have been bad. But most of the runs were for people complaining of various aches and pains that you might be suffering from yourself. These people had no idea what a private doctor was and it was much more convenient to call us than a taxi, not to mention cheaper.

I was called out on Christmas Eve one time at around midnight. We had already done nine or ten runs and we had seven hours to go. When we got to the house there was a man standing at the front door and he looked very disturbed. "I'm so sorry," he said and he repeated it a few times. I thought to myself, uh oh, what did this guy do? I thought maybe he had shot or killed somebody. We went to the front door and he let us in, still wringing his hands and apologizing. "What's the matter," I said as I realized that he was two sheets to the wind. "Well," he said, "first of all I want to tell you that I've been drinking." "Okay," we said, "how long have you been drinking?" "Since Thanksgiving," he replied. Now keep in mind this is Christmas Eve! "Have you been to the hospital?" we asked. "Oh yeah, been there," he said. "Did they give you anything, pills, medicine to take?" "Yeah they sure did," he slurred. "Did you take it?" This was getting to be like pulling teeth. "No I didn't," he said. Of course our next question was why not? "That's why I called you," he said. "I couldn't get the top off!" He went and got the medicine and we took the childproof cap off, wished him a Merry Christmas and went to our next response. Even we had to laugh at that one, but most of the runs were not so funny and as they piled up during the course of the night it got very frustrating. After four 14-hour nights of this you really needed a beer and someone to vent to. Fortunately there was always another firefighter that was willing to have a drink and commiserate with you.

My first experience with a shooting victim came riding the ambulance on September 7, 1972. We were sent to the 900 block of Harlem Avenue for a report of a shooting. When we got there, the police were pulling up at the same time. The shooting took place at the Jumbo Ice Cream store and it was a mess. A man had come in and tried to rob the owners who were working behind the counter. The owners, two half-brothers, pulled their own guns and started blazing away. They exchanged shots with the would-be hold-up man but unfortunately they got the worst of it. They both lay dead on the floor, both shot through the heart. The robber had also been shot but had managed to escape. He was found a few blocks away with a gunshot wound under his arm. He lived and was sentenced to life in prison. I often thought how unlucky the owners were to take two shots to the heart. It was just bad luck that the bullets found their mark. There was no way that the murderer was that good a shot. That only happens in the movies.

I had never liked riding the ambo and eventually it would lead me to start studying for Lieutenant and Emergency Vehicle Driver which would allow me to drive the hook & ladder trucks and get me away from riding the ambulance. It is said that getting off the ambo was the overriding factor in making people study. I don't doubt it in the least. My hat is off to the modern day paramedics who staff the medics in Baltimore city. I wouldn't have their job if you doubled my salary.

When I was detailed, but not riding the ambo, I enjoyed it. It was good to meet the guys you were trying to beat in to their boxes all the time. I spent a lot of time at Engine 13 and Truck 4. Their house was a lot more modern than Engine 25; no second floor for one thing which meant no poles to slide. I never minded the poles but some of the older guys had had enough of them. I saw a number of guys hurt themselves sliding them. Waking up in the middle of the night and sliding a 20 foot pole to a concrete floor could be hazardous to your health. More than once I saw guys let go too soon and drop the last 8 or 10 feet and wind up with a twisted ankle or worse. Of course if you saw this, it was always good for a laugh after you found out they weren't hurt too bad.

I also spent a lot of time at Engine 8 and Truck 10 on Lafayette Ave. Their house was very similar to Engine 13's and the men were very alike also. By that I mean there seemed to be a basic similarity in the attitude of almost all of the men in these busy houses. Of course, there were always some exceptions, but by and large the attitude was the same: I know I'm good at what I do, I like what I do and if you don't like it, that's too bad. I don't mean to convey that they were braggarts or showoffs. Far from it, nobody went around saying "hey look at me and what I'm doing." But they went about their jobs with a self-assuredness that seemed to be missing in some companies.

Every shift in every company was different and it didn't take long to learn who you could depend on and who you couldn't. The men knew, the chiefs knew and some of the talking heads downtown knew it too. If a certain Truck company was dispatched on a fire and they were first in, the men on the second truck knew that they were going to have to work extra hard to make up for the short comings of the first truck. That's the way it was then and it's still that way today. Not all the so-called "good companies" were in busy neighborhoods either. There were a lot of older guys that transferred to the slow houses as their careers wound down. They were content to have a slow night more often than not, but when they did get a "good fire," they were still good firefighters. My problem was with the guys that went to slow houses right out of fire school and never bothered to learn what it took to be a good firefighter. There is nothing like experience to teach you what you should and should not do. I always felt as if there should have been some kind of rotation policy with the companies. Of course, that would have pissed off the guys in the busy houses, who were there precisely because it was busy. And I don't think the guys in the slower houses would have been too happy about it either. I guess it's a good thing I was never in charge.

My times at Engine 25 seemed to be few and far between. With only two of us taking details, I seemed to be on the road most of the time, as details were called a lot. I liked being home at Engine 25 because there was not a company in the city that got more fire than we did. We covered a big area that got a tremendous amount of fires. It was not too long after I got to Engine 25 that my Lieutenant decided that enough was enough and transferred out to a slower house. His replacement was a new Lieutenant who had just been promoted. Lt. Warner came from Engine 14, a very busy single house in West Baltimore, south of Engine 8. He was young and a go-getter who would never let anyone out-work him, no matter if it was in the house or on the fire ground.

On March 2, 1973, we were dispatched to a dwelling fire in the 2000 block of Linden Ave. We were the first Engine in and dropped our lead off line a block away and proceeded up the street. The dwelling was off pretty good and the crowd that had gathered was screaming that there were people inside. Lt. Warner and I advanced a line into the front door and started to crawl down the hallway. We didn't know it at the time but Truck 4, the first Truck in, was having one hell of a time out front. It seems that the man who set the fire didn't want the firefighters to rescue anybody so he was trying to knock their ladders down as fast as they could put them up. The police weren't there yet and the scene outside was chaotic. Meanwhile Lt. Warner finds a man lying in the hallway and hollers to me to hit the fire and he will be right back. I'm lying in the hallway throwing water and taking a beating while he drags the civilian outside. At this time, Jim Sanders, our lead-off man, comes in with a mask on and tells me to take a break. As I exit the building, I see Lt. Warner, who now has the civilian draped across his shoulders, get punched in the chest by the same guy who had been knocking down the ladders. I jumped on the guy and proceeded to knock him down and beat his head into the sidewalk until he was knocked out. This enraged some of the people who were watching the fire and a near riot broke out. Luckily, the police had arrived and one cop, who looked like Bubba Smith, the defensive end for the Colts, told the big mouth in the crowd to shut up and back off. The big mouth wouldn't listen and I watched as the cop whacked him across the mouth with an 18 inch aluminum flashlight. The ambulance took him and the man I had knocked out and the victim the Lieutenant had carried outside to the hospital. It was a good fire that went to two alarms with no loss of life, no thanks to the arsonist. The veterans didn't think twice about what had happened, but I was still a rookie and I was amazed at what had taken place. The fire was our fifth run of the night but our only fire.

When I first came to Engine 25 at McCullough and Gold Streets, I was in culture shock. I had never been to West Baltimore in my life. The west side was predominately black and on the other side of town from where I lived. The violence just amazed me; the shootings, stabbings and beatings were endless. Most of the time, these acts of violence were committed over trivial things and drugs. The thing that bothered me the most was the children. I would watch them watching what was going on around them and think, "these kids don't have a chance." Anybody who grows up in that environment and manages to not succumb to peer pressure or fall into the lifestyle of violence that seems to permeate that neighborhood deserves a huge pat on the back. I honestly don't know if I could have avoided all the pitfalls if I had lived there. I felt sorry for the older people who couldn't get away and were virtual prisoners in their own homes. It shouldn't be that way. I didn't feel sorry for the low-lifes that were causing all of this. When we were called out on the ambo and the victim was a drug dealer, we did our best to save him but if he didn't make it, it was not the end of the world. When children suffered at the hands of these criminals, it left you feeling angry. Angry at the people who did it and angry at the system that let it happen. There must be an answer but I'm not smart enough to figure it out. I just clean up after it.

In April of 1973, I'm driving the ambo as usual, and the attendant is one of the better medics in our firehouse. The thing that stands out in my memory the most about him is his ability to eat chicken legs in just a matter of seconds. He would stick the leg in his mouth and twirl it around and presto, no meat left, just bone. He and I were riding together this day when we get a call to 1300 Druid Hill Ave. It's a large building that has some kind of city agency in it. We go to one of the offices and there is a man lying on the floor, not breathing and with no pulse. This was before HIV was commonly known and understood and before rebreather equipment so I started mouth to mouth while the medic started chest compressions. We worked like hell on this guy for quite some time and he slowly started to come around. We took him to the ambo and worked on him some more. We eventually got him breathing and raced to the hospital. He made a complete recovery and even went back to work a few weeks later. We didn't know it at the time but the police officer on the scene and the victims' co-workers wrote to the fire department and gave a glowing report of the incident. We were given a commendation for a job well done. I did not think we had done anything spectacular but I didn't give the commendation back. It was my first one. To this day, I think commendations are overrated. I've seen guys do some great things on the fire ground and the chief said, "That's just your job." I've also seen engine men take a tremendous beating inside a dwelling keeping the fire from jumping to another room while a truck man puts a ladder up to a balcony and helps a civilian climb down. The truck man gets a commendation and the engine man throws up. No justice.

CHAPTER 4
Different Jobs

The difference between truck work and engine work is like night and day. I did both, 8 years on the engine and 21 years on a truck, so I think I can compare the two fairly. In the engine company, when you are first in there is nothing like it. You leap off the wagon, grab the length of hose you think is appropriate and race for the front door. You make sure you are buttoned up [turnout coat, gloves] and you start in. You must get to the heart of the fire but you also have to keep under the heat. This means crawling on your belly for as long as it takes. You are waiting for the telltale sign that you have water coming. Usually you can feel the hose start to twitch before the water gets there. The closer you get, the hotter it gets and you have to keep your head down so your helmet gives you some protection from the heat. All the while you are doing this, your officer is right up your butt, talking to you. "A little further, that's it keep going, we're getting there." You spot the fire licking out of two rooms at the end of the hallway and head in that direction. "Hit it," your officer says and you open up the nozzle, slowly at first to let the air escape and then full force. Not on a straight stream but on a partial fog pattern. This beats the fire back, gives you some protection and allows you to move forward. "Put it on the ceiling," you're told and that's what you do. One second you can see the fire and the next you can't see two inches in front of you. Your lungs feel like they are going to explode and the snot is running out of your nose like a river but you still have one more room to put out. You back out and turn to the other room. The flames are crawling across the ceiling and licking out the door but your water quickly knocks them back. You get the fire knocked down and head for the nearest window, a quick gulp of air and lay the nozzle on the window sill and open it up. This helps suck some of the heat and smoke out the window. You are dead tired but you know you did a good job and the adrenalin is starting to wear off. As you make your way out to the street you are surprised at how close the rooms are to the front door. You could have sworn you crawled 50 yards down that hallway, not 20 feet. You are wet, tired and dirty but it feels good. Almost every day somewhere in Baltimore a firefighter is doing this and the only recognition he gets is from his peers. That is more than enough.

Truck work is completely different. If you are first in, you know you have to take the front of the building. You must be able to raise your ladders to the windows to ventilate and if you have to, rescue people. The roof has to be opened up; this is done by the driver by raising the aerial ladder for access to the roof. Truck men are not tied down by the hose and they don't have direct supervision. Each man has a job to do depending on the situation and if just one job is done wrong, it can cause someone to lose their life. You must ventilate from the top down, roof, upper windows, etc. If you don't, you can cause a flashover that can incinerate the men inside. You can't open up too soon or you will cause the fire to spread by giving it oxygen before the engineman has water. There always seems to be too many jobs and not enough men to do all the truck work that has to be done. You must go in with the pipe man to pull ceilings and open up the walls; the building has to be ventilated. And first and foremost, you must search for victims. You have to go above the fire most of the time by crawling in a window. You look under beds, behind doors; anywhere someone might have gone to try to escape the heat and smoke. All of this must be done by feel because you are above the fire and the smoke is rising making it impossible to see. You have to try to remember how you got in the room so you can find your way out. You have your mouth on the floor looking for a little pocket of air so you can keep going. If you find someone you have to get them to the window, no easy job if they are a large adult.

I once went up a 24 foot ladder and Terry Ryer from Truck 13, handed an unconscious man across the window sill to me. As I tried to maneuver him onto my shoulder in the thick smoke coming out of the window, I put my arm around his thighs to lock him in. The individual was naked so I was also trying to keep certain things out of my face. As I placed my arm around his thighs, he slipped right off and I was lucky to catch an ankle. I had one hand on his ankle and the other on the top rung of the ladder yelling for help. Marty Loftus came up and between the two of us we got him down. "How in the hell did that happen?" I said. "I thought I had a pretty good grip on him." I looked where we had laid him down to wait for the ambo and it was then I noticed that he only had one leg. He was an amputee and there was no thigh to hold on to. This job is full of surprises!

For the truck men, the best thing about working on the truck is the freedom to do what must be done without an officer at your side. The officer has a lot of other things to do without having to worry about you. Nowhere does experience count more than on a truck company. I think it takes a long time to become a real good truck man and you are going to make mistakes, but you have to remember them and try not to repeat them. I learned a lot just watching and listening to the more experienced men; they had been there and done it time and time again.

It is December of 1972. By this time, I have been in the department for almost a year. I can't believe how fast the time has gone by; it seems like just yesterday that I walked in the door. I've been to more fires than I can count including a number of multi-alarm fires. The largest fire I've been on so far has been 5 alarms at the Druid Park Apartments in the 3000 block of Reisterstown Road. Each alarm consists of four engine companies, two truck companies and a battalion chief. We went on the first alarm and saw plenty of fire blowing out the first floor rear. We advanced our line in and put a good stop on it, or so we thought. After we had the fire out, we were sitting on the rubble inside taking a break when I hollered to a firefighter outside, "have they put the recall in yet?" The recall was what the chief on the fire ground called in to let communications know the fire was under control. "Hell no," he said, "The Chief just pulled a second alarm." He pointed above us, so I looked up and sure enough the floors above us were blazing away. It seems the fire had started in a trash chute and had traveled through the walls. By the time it was over, there were five alarms in and 80 people were homeless.

On January 5, 1973 I experienced my first fatalities in a dwelling fire on Gwynns Falls Parkway near Engine 52. It was not even that big a fire, but it killed four children before we could get it out. I did not see any of them because the truck companies pulled them out and they were rushed to the hospital. We weren't first in and really didn't get to throw much water on the fire at all. After the fire was out and we were overhauling, something happened that I have never forgotten. I was helping to throw out the burned furniture and debris when I noticed a firefighter from Truck 11 looking through a small box. He came up with a handful of money, looked around without seeing me, and shoved the money in his pocket. I didn't know what to do at first, I was still one of the newer guys and this firefighter had been in for a number of years. I thought about it for about five minutes and decided I had to do something. I pulled the guy off to the side where there was no one around and told him I had seen what he had done with the money. I told him to take it back and I would forget I saw it happen, but if he didn't, I was going to the Chief to report it. I regret to this day that I didn't just turn him in right then and there. To steal is bad enough but to steal from a family that had just lost four kids was the lowest you could get. He returned the money and walked away. I told James Schuster about it after we got back to quarters and when he heard who it was he said he wasn't surprised, that the guy was a thief and a low-life. I guess every job has its bad apples but that really turned my stomach. I tried to keep an eye on that guy every time we had a fire with him but it was hard to do. He didn't go inside very often when the fire was still burning which just lowered my already low opinion of him.

On Wednesday, July 11th of that year, we were on night work and it was a slow night. A few false alarms, a pot of food left on the stove, nothing exciting. We had a young guy that used to ride along with us as an auxiliary man. Auxiliary men were not uncommon in the department and they were always nice to have around. They were basically fire buffs that had permission to ride but were not allowed to go inside a dwelling while it was burning. This young guy who was with us that night kept saying, "I'm hanging around because I have a feeling we are going to get a big one tonight." The night went by and nothing happened and finally at around 5:30 in the morning he left. At 5:45 a box was struck out in Hampden, a blue collar neighborhood north of Engine 25, for a report of a super market on fire on Elm Avenue. It quickly went to two alarms and off we went on the second alarm. As we neared Hampden I thought I saw our auxiliary man driving away from the scene but I was not positive.

Upon our arrival, you could see that this was going to be a very big fire before it was through. The entire store was ablaze from top to bottom. It eventually went to eight alarms and culminated with the front of the building collapsing into the street. It was the most spectacular fire I had seen so far, but as I was to learn, there was not a lot you could do except pour water on it from the outside. This is known as a surround and drown, a good time to renew old acquaintances. We got relieved on the fire ground a couple of hours after we got there, but in the afternoon when we reported for night work, we had to go back there. I mentioned to the Lieutenant that I thought I saw our auxiliary man leaving as we were pulling up to the scene that morning. He thought he saw him too, and he walked over and talked to the fire investigation Captain. The Captain asked for his name and let the Lieutenant know that he was aware of this individual and he was under investigation. Nothing ever came of it but I don't remember seeing him around the firehouse after that. They say that arson is the hardest of crimes to prosecute.

CHAPTER 5
Busy Times

Some of the clothing we were issued to fight the fires with was pretty pathetic. The gloves were the same gloves that were given to the trash men. The gloves were made from a material that would actually melt if it got too hot. Our helmets were made of plastic, like a toy helmet you would give to a little boy. They also would melt if you got too close to a fire, something we all did. We used to buy our own helmets that were made of aluminum and were much sturdier. The drawback of having that type of helmet was that if you were fighting a fire in a thunder storm you were like a lightning rod. However, it was still better than what the city gave us. The city always buys from the lowest bidder and you get what you pay for. This was true even when they were buying new engines and trucks. I honestly don't know how some politicians look themselves in the mirror every day. There are some things that you should never skimp on and fire equipment should be at the top of the list. Of course I might be biased on this particular subject. It took a lot of years and a lot of complaining from the union but we did start to get better equipment down the road.

In July of 1973 we were very busy the whole month. Besides the supermarket fire, we had numerous other fires, a lot of which were multiple alarms. Also in July, my wife and I had another son who we named Steve. Now with another mouth to feed and with my wife staying home to be a full time mom, it was time for me to do the same things most firefighters do; it was time to get a second job. In the early days of my career I had marveled at the fire fighters I worked with who would run all night and then go to a second job. I was about to find out what that was like. I drove a truck for a while; I painted for a while and did any other job that required a strong back and a weak mind. I guess your body just gets used to a small amount of sleep and after a time it's part of your routine. I definitely couldn't make it on my fire department salary. $9,000 dollars a year does not go very far with a family of four. I always wondered why the people that shape your children's minds, the people that protect you from criminals and the people who risk their lives trying to save you from fire are among the lowest paid city employees. I do believe society turned things topsy-turvy on me when I wasn't looking. With that said, I would never have left the job for a better paying desk job. I knew after fire school that I had found what I was going to do for at least the next 20 years.

In September of 1973 a new firehouse opened downtown, the John F Steadman Firehouse was the official name for it but it quickly became known as the Super House. It was huge, with room for eight companies and sleeping quarters upstairs. The basement was a high pressure pumping station to serve downtown. As the saying goes, "it must have seemed like a good idea at the time." I spent a lot of time detailed to the Super House. To tell you the truth, when I was there it was one big party. There were too many men and the officers just could not keep track of everybody. At night when the sun went down, most of the officers went in their office and closed the door. In the early 70's drinking on the job was not unusual, some just took it to the extreme. At the Super House there might be two or three parties going on at once after the sun set. High stakes card games were a regular part of the night there and more than once guys would lose their pay check. I never played in the card games but I was known to drink a beer or two while I was detailed there. I never wanted to transfer there though, not enough fire for me. There were a lot of smells and bells downtown but not the working fires that we had in the 4th battalion. But it was fun going down there; a nice change of pace.

On October 4th at a little after 8 pm, an alarm was struck out for a fire in the Strippy Storage & Moving Company in the 100 block of McPhail Street. This was down near Engine 14, well out of our district, but it did not take long to go to a second alarm. We wound up taking it on the fifth alarm and before all was said and done there were nine alarms pulled. It was obvious that the building could not be saved, but there was a paint company that was adjacent to the fire building. The fire roared for three hours and the effort to save the paint company was successful. Another surround and drown, but it is exciting for about the first hour. The big ones are spectacular but it's the one and two alarm fires that are the toughest to fight. At least it was not too cold; some guys would rather fight fires in the winter and not in the summer. Not me, once I get wet I'm going to be cold right to the bone until I'm back at the station and in dry clothes. With almost two years under my belt, I am feeling like a veteran now. My turnout gear is dirty and my helmet has been burned a number of times. The top of my helmet is also twisted from breaking windows with it. All of my gear smells like smoke. I must be a sick puppy I tell myself, I love what I'm doing.

It is now January 1974 and James Schuster and I are playing pool upstairs at around 9 p.m. when I look out the window and see a large column of smoke right around the corner on Druid Hill Avenue. We run for the poles hollering "turn out, turn out" and slide to the first floor. As we pull out of quarters, the Lieutenant is asking for the box to be struck out which will summon the rest of the companies on the first alarm. A three story row house is on fire and it's going good. As we are leading off, we see a man trying to escape the fire leaping from the third floor and landing on a civilian watching the fire. People are screaming and the fire is rolling out the front door. I make my way to the front steps and start to hit the fire in the vestibule first. I get it knocked down and start in. I get into the hallway when my Lieutenant hollers, "it's off behind us again." I turn around and sure enough the vestibule is burning again. The last thing you want is for the fire to get behind you so I hit it with a good stream and turn back to the hallway again. We crawl a short distance and the damn vestibule lights off again. This time I have to crawl back the way I came to hit it one more time and I really drown it this time. We make our way through the living room, pushing furniture out of the way and keep the water flowing at the ceiling. The dining room is also burning and we crawl through it hitting the fire as we go. We are knocking it down pretty good and make our way to the steps leading to the second floor. One good blast from the hose on the second floor and we have caught up with the fire and stopped it from spreading any further. When we are satisfied that it is out I walk back the way I came in to check on why the vestibule would not stay out. I find a 5 gallon gas can behind the door. A 24 year old man was later arrested and charged with arson. It seems he was mad at his ex-wife and decided to burn her out. We were lucky no one was killed. The man who jumped sustained a broken leg and the guy he landed on hurt his back. Because I had found the gas can I had to go to court to testify against the arsonist. He was convicted and given ten years in prison. Not enough as far as I was concerned.

In July of 1974, the sanitation workers went on strike in Baltimore. As the trash piled up the fires started, first in dumpsters, then at the Cold Spring landfill. It was only the beginning. For twelve days the trash and the fires mounted. Now it was not just dumpster fires. The trash had piled up in the vacant buildings and vacant dwellings and was an easy mark for arsonists. Eventually Chief Curtis, the chief of the fire department, had to order double shifts to work the 14 hour night shift. He activated all second line equipment and asked for help from Anne Arundel County. I was detailed to Engine 8 at the time and it was a wild time to say the least. We were responding to one vacant dwelling fire after another and it took a while to get to each one. That meant that each fire had that much more time to get rolling, and roll they did. Chief Curtis reported that between 9 p.m. Thursday and 4 a.m. Friday, there were 235 boxes struck out and more than 200 silent alarms in the city.

Then on July 12, it really hit the fan. The police went on strike, and that's when the looting and rioting started. Not all the police walked, but western district had the highest amount of men go out. West Baltimore was going up in flames while Mayor Schaefer was on television telling everybody the city was calm. Engine 8 never seemed to be able to get back to quarters. As soon as we put up from one fire, we would go to the next. We could often see another fire burning while we were fighting our own. It became common to hear our Battalion Chief on the scene say, "We have a three story dwelling, the fire is through the roof." Asking for help was a lost cause; there was none available. The whole city was busy. We were fighting fires with companies I had never seen before. We fought a fire on Saratoga Street with Engine 10 which was stationed in South Baltimore. When we would get a chance to return, we would eat, change clothes and out the door we would go again. During this time, the longest I can remember staying in quarters was about one hour. Rob Webb, a member of Engine 8 who was off at the time, stopped by and said, "Here, I thought you guys could use this." It was a case of ice-cold beer and his timing was perfect. Rob and I had gone through fire school together and we laughed about this every time we saw each other after that. It was a welcome break. Between Thursday morning and Monday afternoon there were 2,343 alarms of fire, or an average of 32 an hour. We worked our asses off but to tell you the truth we were young and it was exciting. Still, enough was enough and we were glad when it was over.

In early August, I was working night shift at Engine 25. It was early in the evening and we had just sat down to eat when we got a call for a dwelling fire in the 2500 block of Druid Hill Avenue. We could see the smoke as we turned out of quarters and it didn't take us long to get there. As we pulled up out front there was a woman screaming that her kids were in the house on the second floor. Truck 4 was not there yet and we didn't feel as if we could wait, so Lt. Warner and I ran in to search the second floor. The fire was in the back bedroom and you could see it as we crawled into the front room to search. Without a charged line there was no way we could go in the back room, and from the look of things, if they were in there, it was too late. We crawled around in the smoke and heat without finding anyone and as we made our way back to the stairs, I crawled over a red hot box spring. Ordinarily I would not have even noticed it but in my haste to get in the front door I had not taken the time to put my turn-out coat on. A mistake I would not make again. I quickly received first and second degree burns on my arm. The kids were not in the house, they had escaped by the back door. This was my first burn and it was painful, but it healed quickly and I was back to work in no time. Nothing was said about not having a coat on back then and getting burned, it was just considered part of the job. That would change in later years.

Riding the ambo is really starting to get to me. I seem to be spending less and less time at Engine 25 and more and more time on the ambo. When I'm off for my eight days, which comes about once a month, I can be assured that I'll be on the ambo when I get back to work. I will ride Ambulance 4 for four days, then be detailed somewhere in the city for the next four; the idea of keeping the details in the battalion had gone out the window. Then it's back to the ambulance, usually Ambo 15 at Truck 10.

I have worked the ambo for four fourteen hour nights and only had one call that was worthy of an ambulance trip to the hospital, and we were getting between 14 and 20 calls a night! That one call didn't result in the patient going to the hospital anyway. It was my turn to be in charge because I was working with a rookie. We received a call for a stabbing at Pulaski Street and Edmondson Avenue. When we pulled up, there was a man standing on the corner bleeding profusely from the neck. He had a towel wrapped around his neck and the blood was soaking through and forming a puddle at his feet. We rushed over and before we could say anything he said, "I don't want no white mother fucker touching me." I stepped back. I had run into this sort of thing before but not from someone who really needed help. "Let me take a look at it," I said, but he cursed me again. There were no police around so I asked him if he was refusing my service. He cursed me again so I grabbed my partner and we went back to the ambo. I picked up the microphone and said patient refused service, we are back in service and we left. I had no qualms about leaving. I was not about to stay and fight a guy who had been stabbed in a fight, just to bandage him up. When you rode the ambo you had to be prepared to take verbal abuse for the entire shift; not to mention the filth and the stink of some of the places you went into. It was enough to make you sicker than some of the patients claimed they were. I really like Engine 25 but I'm starting to wonder if it is worth staying there when I don't seem to be there that often anyway.

On September 25th, I am back at Engine 25 on day work and it has been a reasonably quiet day; a few false alarms, one pot of food and one mattress fire. As the day winds down, I am looking forward to my wife picking me up at work. We only have one car; I had wrecked my motorcycle, and sometimes our schedules are a little chaotic. I know Lois will be there at 4 o'clock which is when my relief will be in. I get relieved, put my gear away and I am walking to the door when a box comes in for a dwelling fire at 700 Reservoir Street. Engine 25 is first in and we watch them go out the door and head for "the hill," as reservoir hill is called. We are going in the same direction and I can see the smoke in the sky. "Do you want to see what we do at work?" I can sense she is a little apprehensive but she goes along with it. We pull up as the firefighters are going in with the hose. It is a three story row house and there is heavy black smoke blowing out the windows on the third floor. As we are watching, a firefighter comes racing out with a small child in his arms. Two firefighters start mouth to mouth and chest compressions as we watch. The child looks to be a boy around 5 years old and it does not look good. As the ambo pulls up and they take him away I can feel Lois shaking and she says she wants to go. "I don't care if I never see that again," she says as we drive home. Seeing what we do at work is sometimes very upsetting to the average person and sometimes to us as well. It turns out there was another child in the fire, a 2 year old girl, who also died in the fire. Her remains were found on the third floor in what was left of her crib. The fire was confined to one room on the third floor but it seemed to have been burning for a long time before the fire department was notified. Battalion Chief 4 was quoted as saying "somebody fooled around instead of calling in the alarm. The fire in that room had to be burning at least 20 minutes before we arrived." At work the next day I found out from talking to the guys who had been there that civilians were carrying stereo equipment down the stairs as the firefighters were trying to get upstairs to the children. We wondered how anyone could be so uncaring as to not even make an attempt to rescue the children. It boggles the mind.

CHAPTER 6
Engine 13

I have made up my mind to transfer to Engine 13, right down the street. Things have changed at Engine 25 and not for the better. There is a different Captain of the house who is very lax about everything. Things are not getting done around the house that should be done, especially on his shift. This leaves more of the housework and equipment maintenance around the firehouse to the other shifts and leads to more complaining among the men. I have a chance to stay on "C" shift and go to Engine 13 and I'm going to take it. I will not get detailed as much and a lot of the details will be right in the same house, on Truck 4. I know everybody on the engine and the truck and I always enjoy myself there except when I'm on the ambo. That is another factor in my decision to transfer; I will only have to ride Ambo 4, not Ambo 15. It was a good 2 1/2 years at Engine 25. I learned a lot and met some great guys but I think it's time to move on.

I'm now at Engine 13 and I can tell I'm going to really like it here. For one thing it's a double house, more guys, more room, and more fun. I took the place of a firefighter who was run out of the house by the Captain. This firefighter, at one time, was the driver of Truck 4 on C-shift. A few months earlier there was a fire in the 1900 block of Eutaw Place. It was a big three story row house and it was really going good when we pulled up. I was on Engine 25 and we left room at the front of the building for Truck 4 to pull in. However, the firefighter in question was driving Truck 4 and he was known to drink a lot although he covered it up pretty well. For some unexplained reason, he parked the truck across the street from the fire building. Eutaw Street is three lanes wide so he was parked a long way from the roof of the fire building. That part of the street is also a steep uphill grade. We were inside fighting the fire with the officer of Truck 4 and the place was really off. You could hear the glass breaking and the flames just didn't want to go out. In the middle of all this, Battalion Chief Smith comes in and says in a very quiet voice, "Lieutenant you might want to go outside, your truck just rolled down Eutaw Street and crashed into Truck 11."

It seems that the driver had parked the truck and didn't use the air brake to hold it on the hill, just the manual parking brake. He also had failed to put down the chocks. He had raised the aerial ladder and extended it across Eutaw Street onto the roof. When the brake failed to hold, the truck started rolling down and across the street right towards Truck 11. Truck 11 was parked there because it was a straight body truck and would not fit in the alley in the rear. The men had carried their tools around back and were not on the truck.

Truck 4 made quite a racket as it rolled down the street dragging the jacks underneath of it until it slammed into the front of Truck 11. The aerial ladder had scraped across the roof of half a dozen houses but stayed up. The chief probably should have pulled a second alarm but he didn't and we worked for hours overhauling the debris. Rescue 1 had to be called to jack Truck 4 up to get the ground jacks out from under it, and pull it out of the windshield of Truck 11. I later heard Chief Smith say, "the only way this could be worse is if we have a rekindle." Later that night that's just what we had. The driver was found guilty of numerous charges and part of his punishment was a reduction in rank to firefighter and a transfer from Truck 4 to Engine 13. Captain Graleski was not happy about this and vowed to put him on charges if he even smelled like he was drinking. He advised the firefighter to transfer to another company and he did. This created an opening on Engine 13 and I put my transfer in and it was granted. It was a move I would not regret.

We had a wonderful collection of men on C-shift. Some of the funniest guys I had ever met were all on one shift. It didn't matter what color or religion, everyone was open to ridicule. Practical jokes were an everyday occurrence and if you couldn't laugh at yourself you might as well transfer. We played cards day and night. Ping pong, basketball and volleyball games were always going on. We had a great blend of young and old and a lot of us started hanging together in our off time. These guys could fight some fire too. Trying to keep them from going into a burning building was like trying to put a leash on a mad pit bull. We partied hard and we worked hard and I don't think there was a better shift in a better house in the city. Stan Williams was on our shift and he was a big guy, 6'4 about 230 lbs. and he could do the best gay guy impression I've ever seen. We had a painter come in to decide what color to paint the interior of the house and it was obvious that he was gay. When Stan went into his act I saw this guy's eyes light up and I knew it was love at first sight. He followed Stan around for days while we were laughing so hard it hurt. Doug Falls was also there, the guy from fire school who never stops talking. He was still talking non-stop and he would say anything to anybody no matter their rank, but the way he would say things you just had to laugh, even if you were the butt of his jokes. The whole shift was full of characters that I don't think has ever been assembled anywhere else. I couldn't wait to go to work every day. We fought fires and laughed, played cards and laughed, and life was good.

In the later part of 1974, shortly after I transferred in to Engine 13, we seemed to have a rash of mattress fires. Most of these would be handled by the first engine and truck on the scene, but they were nasty fires. We would crawl into the bedroom, dragging a small one inch booster line and find the mattress. You would put just enough water on it to darken it down and then roll it up as best you could and throw it out the window. The smoke was a nasty, snot rolling, stick in your throat kind of smoke. It was the best way to clear up a congested nose in the shortest time imaginable.

Another kind of fire that was common was the pot of food. Food left unattended on the stove that never really catches fire, it just burns all the food and the pan it is in and fills the house up with smoke. It could be the best steak or hot dog but after it burns up it all smells the same. This smoke might be worse than a mattress fire. It clings to your hair, your clothes, the roof of your mouth and your sinuses. Most of the time, there is someone home but they are sleeping and you have to wake them up and get them out. I did have a fatality once on a pot of food but it was not something that happened very often. When we would pull up on the scene, unless it was a working fire, you could tell what was burning by the smell. I remember being amazed when I was a rookie that guys would be able to tell what we had when we were sometimes a block away. They would tilt their head and sniff and declare "pot of food" and I would wonder how they did that. Now it is something I do without even thinking about it. Later in my career we had a pot of food and when we got into the hallway we could hear rap music playing loud enough to wake the dead. We banged on the door and got no answer so I kicked the door in and we went inside. There were two guys passed out on the couch and the pot was smoking away in the kitchen. We checked to make sure the sleepers were breathing ok and turned off the stove and threw the pot out. We tried to wake them up but it was useless so we left one of our cards that says we were here and got ready to go. I leaned over as we were leaving and changed the channel on their radio to a country station and left the volume up. I would like to have been a fly on the wall when they woke up. Sometimes this job is just too much fun!

I get detailed to the Truck a lot more now and I'm really starting to appreciate the work that they do. It is more physically demanding and you are on your own a lot, which I like. I know when I'm on the pipe and we are crawling down a hallway and the heat and smoke lift a foot or two off the floor, that the truck men have done a good job opening up. Raising the 35 foot wooden ladder is a lot of work and has to be done by three guys. One day I saw the 35 get loose from the men as they were trying to raise it in high winds on a rainy day. It looked like a giant redwood falling. It landed on a parked car and caved the roof in.

Fred Hill was the tiller man on Truck 4 and I would watch him work the back of the truck, swinging it out on the tight turns and then back again. I thought that someday I would like to have that job. Truck work was different but to me there was still nothing like riding the pipe and being first in on a working fire. Of course, if you were not first in you had to lead off and take the rear, dropping hose all the way, and there was a good chance you would not get to throw any water on the fire anyway.

One of my first fires on Engine 13 was a two-alarm fire in the 500 block of Eutaw Street. We took it on the first alarm but Engine 7 was first in. Captain Graleski, myself and a new guy named Mike Ellis, detailed from Engine 7 to Engine 13, went in the back door. For a change, we all had air masks on as we started up the back stairs. The fire was on all three floors but most of it was in the front. As we got near the top, the Captain lost his footing and fell back down the steps, breaking the connection to his regulator on the air bottle. He hollered for me to take the new guy and search the upstairs. We went into a bedroom on the second floor and started feeling around; you couldn't see much, the smoke was too thick. I crawled across what felt like a bed and searched the other side of the room. As I crawled back across the bed, I noticed that it didn't feel right to me. I put my face down real close to the bed to get a better look and I stared right into the face of a very big woman. She was lying on her back and she was unconscious. I yelled for Mike to give me a hand and we tried to pick her up but she was just too heavy. I told him to go find some more guys so we could get her out of there. He ran across the room but unfortunately he missed the doorway and hit the wall. He composed himself and went out the door and came back with three more guys. We managed to get her out and down the steps and out onto the sidewalk. She was taken to the hospital and survived. It turned out that she had set the fire and then she laid down and covered herself up with newspapers. She was being evicted that day and decided to end it all. It was a good fire and my mother, who worked downtown, saw most of it from across the street. We all had a good time with the new guy for running into the wall but he did do a good job. He later went on to become the Captain of Truck 16 for many years.

When the cold months would roll around, the fires would pick up; not that there was a shortage of fires in West Baltimore in the summer. Of course, we didn't get a fire everyday but we definitely got more than our share. When we were not fighting fires on day work, there was house work to be done and our Captain was a stickler for house work. He once took the heating element out of the oven because the oven was not clean enough. We couldn't cook for a week but he had made his point. He took a house that was once the dumping ground for wayward firefighters and turned it around. Not an easy job when you are butting heads with headquarters. After he got the men he wanted on his shift, he backed off a little but not much. It took a while but he wound up in the card games and was even the butt of some of Doug Falls' never ending commentary. We would play pitch for hours on end and at the end of the day not much more than two or three dollars would change hands but the laughter never stopped. I was convinced that it couldn't get any better than this.

On Sunday, November 17th, we were on night work and had just finished dinner. The card game was just about to start when communications dispatched box 867, Eutaw and Ducatel Street, for a report of a dwelling fire in the 2300 block of Eutaw Street. We sprint for the engine, hop on and out we go, making a right out of quarters and a left onto Eutaw Street. We know we are going "up the hill" where there is always a good chance of a working fire. We also know that we will be taking the rear because Engine 25 will be first in. As we cross North Avenue, we can see heavy smoke in the sky. We scream by the front of the dwelling as Engine 25 is stopped in front of the dwelling and pulling their line off. I take a quick look at the front of the dwelling and I can see flames rolling out the third floor windows and blowing well above the roof line. I look at Stan, who is sitting across from me, and give him a thumbs up. This looks like it could be an all-nighter. We have to go up to the top of the street and make a left and find a hydrant to lead off from. We spot a hydrant and drop Stan to lead off. I get on the back step and we start down the trash filled alley to take the rear. The 2 ½ inch lead-off line is flying off the back of the pumper as we make our way to the rear of the dwelling.

The house on fire is a huge three story row house, typical of most of the houses up on the hill. The flames are blowing out the third floor in the back as much as they are blowing out the front. We pull up behind Truck 11 and pull our 1 1/2 inch line off and start up the sidewalk. As we near the back door, I look over and two men from Truck 11 are bending down next to a civilian who is lying on the concrete next to the dwelling. I can see what looks to be his brains and blood everywhere around him, but I don't stop, they can handle him, I have to get our line in service. We get inside on the first floor with no problem and make our way to the stairway leading to the second floor. As the water makes its way up to the nozzle, I look up the stairs and all I can see is fire; the walls, the ceilings and even the steps themselves are fully engulfed in flame. We get buttoned up and start up. As we get closer, I open the nozzle, take a big gulp of air, get down on my stomach and in we go. I've never been in this much fire at one time. I've got the hose wide open and it does not seem to be having any effect. I get stopped dead in my tracks, feel as if I'm about to burst into flames and finally have to back down a few steps.

At about this time another engine company comes in with us and we decide to go up together, side by side. We are lucky it is a wide enough stairway that we can do this. We make our way up and into the fire again but this time with two lines going at once we are making headway. Together we battle our way up onto the third floor which is nothing but flame. Every room is on fire and it's up in the ceiling. Charles Forte, from Truck 4, appears next to me and starts to pull the ceiling down, almost right on top of us. Again it is nothing but fire all the way to the roof. A second alarm has been struck out and then a third and fourth in quick succession. The fire has spread to the dwellings on either side of this one and other companies are trying to stop the fire from going any farther. After what seems like an eternity, we can see that we have knocked the worst of it down, at least in our building. I need a break so I hand the line to Stan and follow it back down the way we came in. The stairs we came up are partially burned away, as are the railings. It almost seems impossible that we came up that way now that I look at it. I exit out the front door just to take a look around.

All of Eutaw Street is filled with apparatus, from one end of the block to the other. Two and one-half inch hose is thick in the street and lines are stretched into all three houses. Thirty-five foot ladders are thrown to all three houses and the front of the original fire building is burned black past the roof line. Wow, I think to myself, that was a hell of a fire. The civilian that was lying in the back had leaped from the third floor and landed on his head. He was dead on arrival at the hospital. There were eight children and six adults in the house when the fire broke out; they all made their way out except for him. He was on the third floor and had made his way down but went back up because he thought that one of the kids was still up there. We were there for most of the night and it felt good to get back to quarters and get cleaned up and put dry clothes on. I scratched from my part-time job and slept in the next day. When I awoke the next day, my body felt like it did after a football game. This job can really take its toll on you; I don't see how some of the older guys do it.

My kids are growing up quickly, Ray is now four and Steve is going on two. Working two jobs I don't get to see them as much as I would like but I know that having Lois home all the time is the best thing to do. As soon as is possible she says she is going to find a part-time job. She is an excellent secretary and should have no problem finding a job. We live in a small two story row house in the city and the neighborhood is going downhill fast. I don't think this will be the best place to raise our children but we can't afford to move right now. Ray got hit by a car the other day riding his bike in the alley behind our house but he jumped right up and was unhurt. I saw the whole thing happen and it was his fault but my heart was in my mouth when it happened. Fatherhood is a scary but wonderful experience. I look forward to the little league years and I can't wait. I feel very lucky.

CHAPTER 7
A Different View

There is only one constant in the fire department and that is change. Everything changes, men transfer in, men transfer out, men get promoted and leave and some retire. In November of 1974, the 4th Battalion changed. No companies moved, there was just a shuffling around. The new 4th now consists of Engines 13, 1, 7, 18, 38, Trucks 4 and 11 along with Ambulances 4 and 16 and Battalion Chief 4. It really does not affect us much; we were running with these companies all the time anyway. It just means that if I'm detailed to a house in my own battalion, it will not be Truck 10 or Engine 52 anymore. Our shift has not changed much and I'm glad of that.

Our company also handles the manning of the red car. That is the common name for the chief's car which has a driver assigned to it. When the driver is off, we supply a man to drive. I've been approved to do that now and it's not a bad job for a change of pace. The driver does not have to pull watch desk duty but of course he also does not get to fight the fires either. One of his responsibilities is to go to the rear of the burning dwelling and advise the chief by radio what the situation is. It is a very different view of what is going on at a fire. I'm used to just seeing my own little view of the fire, such as a long hallway and a room full of fire. Now I get to see the overall picture and it is an eye-opener. First of all, you get to see who is doing the right things and who is not. You see who is goofing off and who is busting their ass. For instance, I might see an Engine company take the hose and stick it in the window while there are men making their way into the dwelling. This is something that should almost never be done, yet I've seen it happen on more than one occasion. By sticking the hose in the window not only do you block the smoke and heat from escaping from that window but you are also blowing the fire back onto the men coming in the front. I've seen men take out windows before there is a charged hose line in place, thereby spreading the fire with the influx of oxygen. I am thankful that James Schuster, Jim Sanders, and my officers at Engine 25 taught me the right way to do things. I will try to pass on what I have learned to any new guys that join our company, but I know I still have a lot to learn.

The days and nights pass by quickly but the fires never stop. We have fought more fires than I can count over the last month; dwellings, buildings, multiple alarms, and mattress fires. Throw in the numerous false alarms and what I call nuisance runs and we keep pretty busy. Nuisance runs are all the things we get called out for that any rational human being would not call the fire department to handle. We go out for the toilet over flowing and cut the water off, blown fuses, a trace of water in the basement, leaking pipes, the list is endless. We are jacks of all trades but the master of one. We are also the only city agency that the people can call and know that they will get service right away. The nuisance calls are a pain in the ass but it is still better than riding the ambo. We were called out a few days ago for water in the basement of an apartment building. It was almost right next door to the firehouse and we had been there numerous times before. We went inside and walking to the basement door, we could hear the water running. When I shone my light down the stairs, I could see that the water was at least knee deep. "I'll go down and turn the water off," I said. I pulled my ¾ boots up and went down. The water was almost over the top of my boots and I had to walk carefully so as not to get it inside my boot. I walked about 4 steps when, to my disgust, I realized that all around me was human excrement. I hollered upstairs to let them know not to come down and walked even more carefully back to the steps. It goes without saying that everybody avoided me until I could get outside and hose myself off. That is just part of the glory of being a firefighter!

I once watched a rookie take the cover off a malfunctioning smoke detector only to have about 100 cockroaches fall on his head. He screamed like a little girl and we laughed like madmen. When we went to the Murphy Homes we would not lean up against the walls because you didn't want to bring any hitchhikers back to the firehouse. One day Engine 8 and Truck 10 had a mattress fire and when they got back to their quarters they discovered that they were all covered with lice and mites. Their clothes, the apparatus, their hair, everything was infected. The companies were shut down for the night to be fumigated and the men showered and were sent to other houses to finish the night. One of the guys being sent to Engine 13 was a tall, loud, very funny firefighter named Mason Smith, who was actually from Engine 38. When we heard he was being sent over to us we drew a line on the floor and told him to keep his bug infested ass on his own side of the line. We all got a big kick out of it, including Captain Graleski. Later in the evening the Captain was at the watch desk with his back turned to the large glass window that faced the apparatus floor. Unknown to the Captain, Smitty went over to the window, bared his ass, put it up against the window and knocked on it. When the Captain turned around he was looking right up Smitty's ass. "Hey Cap, you see any bugs up there?" Smitty yelled. We were falling down laughing as was our Captain. Things are never dull at our house.

It's Saturday, January 18, 1975. We are on night work and it has been a busy night. No fires of any consequence - a dumpster fire, a pot of food, numerous false alarms and water leaks. Enough to keep us up most of the night but it is now 5:30 a.m. and everybody is in bed except the man on watch. Another half hour and our reliefs will start to roll in. Suddenly the bunkroom lights come on and the gong bangs itself to life. Turn out, everybody goes, second alarm, 2900 Walbrook Avenue. The 2900 block of Walbook is out West North Avenue, almost behind Engine 20 and Truck 18. The block is all three story row houses and one of them must be really burning at this time in the morning. We arrive on the scene and are told to take our line around back and into the adjacent dwelling. There seems to be pandemonium out front but we don't have time to find out why. It is obvious that we have fire in the house next door, thick black smoke is pouring out the third floor windows. We make our way up to the third floor along with Truck 4. The hose is charged and is being pulled up the stairs by all hands. At the top of the stairs I see the fire blowing out of one room. We crawl in along with the Truck men and go to work. We quickly knock it down and the ceilings get pulled to check for extension. We know that the bulk of the fire was next door and that Engine 20 and Truck 18 must have really had their hands full for a while.

We all sit down where we are and take a break, cigarettes are lit and derogatory comments are soon being exchanged. We are dirty and wet but that does not stop us from laughing at each other. Suddenly a firefighter appears in the doorway and tells us to keep it down, "They can hear you all the way out front," he says. "So what?" we answer, "We're not hurting anything." "You assholes, they have eight people dead next door, most of them children." Oh hell, we didn't know, and the mood immediately changes. It's not our fault that we did not know but I can't help but think what it must have sounded like to the relatives outside. I want to holler out the window that we didn't know but I know it is useless.

Five children and three adults have died, all related to each other in one way or another. When Engine 20 first arrived, flames were shooting out ten feet past the windows on the second floor and extending to the third floor. Four of the victims were found in a second floor bedroom, two were found in the second floor rear bedroom and one was found in the third floor bedroom. The last victim was not found until the debris was cleared away after part of the third floor collapsed. In all, three alarms were struck out and it was a very bad night. We stood at our third floor window and looked down on the family members gathered in the street. The looks on their faces were not something I would be able to put out of my mind for a long time. After we were relieved on the fire ground and got back to quarters, I cleaned up and went home. The first thing I did was go into my sons' rooms and hug them. Life is precious and we sometimes lose sight of that. That night was a grim reminder.

Ray Lockett, Bob Sledgeski, and Jim Miller with a 2 1/2 inch hose on the Herculese Ship Building Fire. (Unknown)

CHAPTER 8
Volunteers

We had a man detailed to the Truck the other day who was also a volunteer firefighter in Baltimore County. For the life of me, I will never understand how anyone can justify doing that. I can see a need for volunteers in the rural areas, but not in what has become an urban area like most of Baltimore County. Let me put it this way. If I was a plumber and I had a job to do and you were a plumber and you came to my job site and told the boss, "You don't have to pay him, I'll do it for free," I would be very upset. That is how most paid professional firefighters that I know feel. If they did not volunteer, the spot would in all likelihood be filled by a paid man. This man could be the man who is currently doing it for nothing. Harford County is another example. The entire fire department is volunteers. Fire protection, especially during the day-time, is pitiful. Why not carry it a step further and have a volunteer police department?! The powers that be won't do that because it's a matter of life or death. Well, what do they think the fire department is? Response time is critical in the fire service. It may sound melodramatic but it's true, I have seen many instances where a matter of seconds meant the difference between a life being saved or lost. To me, being a member of the International Firefighters Union and also being a volunteer is hypocritical. I can understand why people don't want to pay more taxes but if it's your house on fire and your loved one inside and you are waiting for a volunteer to leave work and respond to your house, well, all I can say is, you get what you paid for. I will now step down off my soap box.

Towards the end of winter in 1975, we go about a month and our shift has not had a major fire. No shortage of fires but no big blazes. The night of March 3rd would end that. March 3rd was a bitter cold night, well below freezing with gusty winds and sleet. At 9:30 p.m., a night watchman at the J. S. Young Company discovered a fire. The fire was in an unused brick warehouse and machine shop located on Boston Street in Southeast Baltimore. The first Company on the scene reported a working fire and it took off from there. More alarms were struck out in quick succession and we took it on the sixth alarm. We arrived on the scene and it was obviously a surround and drown. We placed our deck gun on the ground near a cut-through between two buildings. The buildings were on the water and the wind was blowing right in our faces, the sleet felt like needles hitting you. We got to the scene at around 10 p.m. and we were there all night. It was the coldest I've ever been since I've been in the department. I had icicles hanging from my helmet, my coat, and my mustache.

While we were there, a two alarm fire broke out in West Baltimore on Beechfield Avenue. At almost the same time, another two alarm fire was going on in the 800 block of Cold Spring Lane in East Baltimore. This prompted the fire department to institute its disaster plan and call on neighboring fire departments to handle some calls. It was a long, cold night. I thought to myself, "I bet it will be a long time before we fight another fire on the waterfront like this one." I could not have been more wrong!

The next night, we were back on night work and still feeling the effects of the all-nighter on Boston Street. At midnight, two police officers reported a fire in a building on the 1400 block of Key Highway. Within eight minutes, six alarms were pulled and we were on our way on the fifth alarm. When we got there, a vacant building was fully engulfed in flames and it had spread to a fuel oil company. The vacant building was formerly the Hercules Ship Building Company and flames were shooting 20 feet in the air. Aided by a brisk wind, the fire spread quickly to the offices of the Atlantic-Richfield and Southern Fuel Oil Company. There were three 500,000 gallon fuel tanks on the premises but they turned out to be empty. Of course the risk of explosion was still high because of the fumes. It was really touch and go for a while, both fireboats were in use and before it was said and done ten alarms had been struck out. Fifty off-duty firefighters had been called back to man reserve apparatus and three companies from Baltimore County and five Companies from Anne Arundel County were placed in stations around the city. A dozen fuel oil trucks were moved away from the oil company and placed on Key Highway. Chris Foster, Mitch Johnson and I held a 2½ inch hose line all night. It was another long, cold night and we were once again relieved on the fire ground. The fire was believed to be arson but no one was ever arrested. I might not get warm for a month!

CHAPTER 9
Good Times

I really enjoy our down time in the firehouse. The card games go on all night and the different personalities are a joy to watch and listen to. At any given time, there are between five and seven guys playing, and the yelling and laughing can be heard all over the house. One of the men on Truck 4 is named Bob Smalls. He was a small black man, about ten years older than me and a real good firefighter. When he would get a real good hand of cards in pitch and thought he could beat everybody at the table, he would stand up and start playing his cards one at a time. If he succeeded in sweeping the hand, he would lean back and act like he was mowing us all down with a machine gun.

Mitch Johnson was the first acting Lieutenant on Engine 13. Mitch was quite a few years older than most of us but as I found out early on, age is not even thought of in the firehouse. We are all friends and colleagues and depend on one another in some tight spots. Mitch has been around for quite a few years and if we have a slow night, he is not disappointed but when the gong goes off, he is right there crawling down the hallway with us.

Another member of Truck 4 is a big blonde haired guy named Charles Forte or Chuck to all of us. He is frugal, and losing a few dollars in a night gets to him, but he is a good card player and does not lose often. He also is easy to deceive and one of our best con games was played on him. He was engaged to get married to a beautiful girl we had all met. He was still relatively new in the job and we told him that he could not get married without the permission of the Chief of the Fire Department. At first he did not believe us but we insisted that anyone in the job had to submit a special report asking permission to marry. We even went so far as to make up a bogus copy of a report asking permission to marry from another firefighter's file. We also convinced him that he had to arrange a date for his bride-to-be to be interviewed by the Chief. He fell for it hook, line, and sinker. He labored over the special report; it had to be done exactly right, her name, date of the ceremony and any other pertinent facts. When he was finished, he was ready to send it through the proper channels, starting with his officer, but we convinced him that it would be better to hand carry it to the Battalion Chief's office, which was also in our house. The Chief was Kenny Henderson, a no nonsense type of Chief, who kept to himself a lot. When Chuck knocked on his door we gathered around the outside of the door. "Here's my special," he said. "What special would that be?" Chief Henderson asked. "My special requesting permission to get married and the dates my wife is available to be interviewed by the Chief of the Department," Chuck replied. Chief Henderson read it, looked at him, read it again and said "Boy, don't you know when somebody is pulling your leg, get out of here." When Chuck walked out, we were all waiting there, laughing and giggling like a bunch of school kids. He took it well and was the subject of conversation for weeks around the rest of the Battalion. I really like being in a double house better than a single house, so much more to do and twice the number of men to interact with.

That same month on the 27th, I am on night work but I'm driving Engine 13. I would much rather be on the pipe but we all have to take our turn filling in as pump operator. Some guys enjoy doing it but I'm not one of them. I do like driving and I feel as if I am a good driver, and I have no problem getting water and supplying the lines, but not going in and fighting the fire irritates me. It is early evening and we haven't really settled into our routines when a box is struck out for a fire in Southeast Baltimore. A second alarm is quickly asked for and this gets our attention. We don't go way over there unless it is a very big fire but the way things have been burning this month, you never know. A third and a fourth alarm are struck out and now I'm looking up on the map to find the best way to get there. According to the run cards, we will take it on the sixth alarm and I don't like to have my officer look for the best way to get there while we are on the street. It does not take long and the fifth and sixth alarms are asked for, and out the door we go.

It's a long response and I enjoy driving in and out of the city traffic, lights flashing, siren screaming, always thinking one car or one traffic signal ahead. When we pull up to the scene, I can't believe what I'm looking at. I have to look twice. I'm looking at the bottom of the fire department water tower. It is cocked up in the air on one side of its jacks and the top of it, where the bucket is, has collapsed onto the roof of a row house. We report to the Chief in charge and are told where to go to hook up to a hydrant and to pump to numerous lines. We do this and after the initial work of hooking up and distributing the water, I have time to see what is burning.

The fire is in a city-owned building that manufactures bags and it is burning through the roof. I know we will be here for at least a couple of hours and I wonder how the man that was in the bucket when it fell is making out. Later I find out that he was in the bucket 90 feet up when it started to sway back and forth. The tower is designed to not topple over but as it continues to rock back and forth, it is apparent that it is going over. If it falls in one direction, it will fall into the fire building. If it falls in the other direction, it will land on a dwelling. As good luck would have it, it falls on the house and the extension arm of the boom snaps over the roof and the operator rolls out of the bucket and onto the roof. Miraculously he is unhurt but I can only imagine how scared he was!

Later an investigation by the manufacturer can come up with no reason for it to have fallen over. The fire department is not sure if it can be repaired and I don't know if I would want to go back up in it if it was! We spend the next couple of hours bailing water on the fire until it is out and we are told to put up and go back to our quarters. As we return to quarters, I realize we still have seven hours to go on this night and we could very well catch another fire before we are done. We get back, clean up and eat a very late dinner and I decide to try to get a few hours rest.

At 2:50 a.m., about two hours after our return from the bag factory call, the gong goes off and the lights in the bunk room come on waking me up and jump starting my heart. "Turn out, second alarm, Greenmount and North Avenue," the man on watch yells. I don't have to look this one up to see where we are going. It's not far and it is a major intersection; one of the worst corners in the city for drugs and violence and I'm not surprised that there is a fire there. The fire is in an alcoholics' halfway house called The Just House. It is a three building complex in the 400 block of East North Avenue. As we are pulling up, I can see Truck men rescuing people from windows on the second and third floor. We go to the nearest hydrant we can find and I again hook up and start pumping. I have time to watch the fire as many lines are stretched into the building and an attempt is made to attack the fire from the inside. This attempt fails and the companies are forced to back out and start the process of surround and drown. Two more alarms are requested, bringing the total to four alarms. As the fire is slowly extinguished and the night drags on, I can see that almost everyone on this fire is dragged out. Just about every company here was also at the bag factory fire and the combination of a six alarm fire and a four alarm fire has taken its toll on everybody.

I actually feel pretty good, aside from lack of sleep. Driving and pumping is not at all like fighting the fire first hand. We return to quarters at 5:30 a.m. and wait for the incoming shift. The Engine is black with soot and all the hose is wet, plus I had failed to fuel up during the night and the tank is well below half full. My relief will not be a happy camper today but I just didn't think of refueling in the middle of the night. Next time we have a night like this I will remember to fuel up between fires.

On my way home, I pass by the scene of the last fire and I can't help but think of the good job everybody did while the city was sleeping. Most of our work takes place in bad neighborhoods and at late hours and it seems as if it goes on without the public knowing about it. That's okay, I tell myself, I know the good job that is done every night here in Baltimore fighting the fires and I'm proud to be a part of it.

CHAPTER 10
Twenty-Four Hours of Fire

In the 24-hour period up to and preceding the bag factory fire, the number of fires in Baltimore City fought by firefighters was staggering. The following is from the Box 414 Association's newsletter called *General Alarm.*[1]

> "Just past midnight, as a full moon shone on the Mt. Vernon-Mt. Royal area of Baltimore, an arsonist got high on brightness. At 12:35 a.m. fire equipment, responding to an alarm, rushed to a fire in a three-story apartment house at 1118 St. Paul Street. It was plainly the work of an arsonist who poured, then ignited, gasoline in a closet beneath a stairway. Controlling this blaze didn't take long. While it was being done however, there came a report of another fire a block away. A Battalion Chief sent one of his men from the first fire to investigate. Flames and smoke were pouring from an apartment house, with people hanging out of the third floor windows. The man sounded an alarm; equipment came and rescued everyone. When they entered the building they saw clear evidence of arson. As a Deputy Chief supervised their work, he saw smoke rising over rooftops three blocks away. Fire equipment, including some which were at the second blaze, rushed there, to the eight story 101 East Apartment House where, again because of obvious arson, it was necessary to ring a second, third and fourth alarm. In the midst of this activity, firemen were told that smoke was coming from a building two blocks away at 1101 St. Paul Street. But a man, sent to investigate, found no fire. Three minutes later, however, an alarm came from another part of the city; from Presstman St. near Druid Hill Avenue. One of the engines which rushed there broke down a block from its destination and its crew ran to the fire scene. Five minutes after that, Fire Headquarters learned that the blaze which had not been found at 1101 St. Paul Street was raging at 1301 in the nine-story Earl Court Apartments. That was at 2:33 a.m. At 3:03 a.m. fire was discovered in the Avon Apartments on Read St. near Charles. Before attacking it, firefighters had to evacuate about 50 persons. And at 3:27 a.m. two members of the department, riding in the vicinity, saw smoke coming from a four-story apartment house at 817

1 Written by members of Box 414 Association (1975, April) Unholy Thursday, 1975. *General Alarm.* Reprinted by Azrael, L. (1975, April 29) Fearsome Night For Firemen. *The News American, pp 7B*

> N. Charles St. The men who rushed there helped ten occupants down ladders to safety. This fire, too, was plainly arson. About an hour later the tragedy of the night occurred about three miles from central Baltimore. Responding to an alarm, firefighters went to a fire in a two-story row house on Woodbourne Ave. It took a half-hour to reduce the blaze sufficiently to enable them to enter. They found the bodies of five children and two adults. Three other adults were removed, suffering from smoke inhalation and heat. This fire was not the work of an arsonist; it started because someone was careless with a cigarette. Dawn brought some respite. But that evening a bag factory in South Baltimore was afire. Tons of burning burlap made thick clouds over the area. And as firemen worked, their huge "snorkel" toppled over, its basket landing on the roof of a house. One man was injured. Six alarms and the help of the fire boat were required to extinguish this blaze, which also appeared to be arson. All of these events took place within less than 24 hours."

Louis Azrael wrote a column in *The News American,* dated April 29, 1975, which he titled "Fearsome Night For Firemen." In the article, he ended by saying "many persons think firemen spend most of their time lolling or playing pinochle in engine houses. It is a pity they were not members of the department during this period." To this I can only add that fires go on every night in Baltimore, of course not that many in a 24-hour period, but dwelling fires occur almost on a daily basis. The average citizen has no idea what we are doing day in and day out.

CHAPTER 11
Taking a Break

On April 22nd, we went on the second alarm of what turned out to be four alarms at a door warehouse in the 800 block of West Fairmount Ave. The fire was through the roof when we got there and Captain Graleski told us to put the 2½ inch line in service. Stan Williams and I got the line in service and we were bailing water on the fire when a Deputy Chief came over and told us to take the line and give it to one of the Truck companies to supply their ladder pipe. We did as we were told and the Captain told both of us to walk back to the engine that was pumping a hydrant three blocks away and take a break.

We walked back and shed our coats and sat down on the back step of the engine. It was now around 1:30 in the morning and we noticed that a bar down the street was still open. We looked at each other, looked at the bar, and thought "what the hell, the Captain said take a break." We walked in the bar and not surprisingly we were the only white guys in there. We placed our helmets on the bar, ordered two beers, and said hello to everybody. When the cans of beer came, Stan told the bartender not to open them. "You can open mine," I said as I looked at Stan like he had suddenly lost his mind. "No don't" he said to the bartender, "just give us a can opener." We were given the can opener and Stan said watch this. He proceeded to make a hole in the side of the can, near the bottom, then turned the can up to his lips and pulled the pull-tab. In a matter of seconds the beer rushed out of the can and down his throat. I was amazed, I had never seen this before. I did the same thing with the same results and we ordered two more. We did it again, much to the amazement of the customers, paid for the beers, said goodnight, picked up our helmets and walked out.

The process of drinking like that was called shot-gunning a beer. It is amazing what you learn in this job. We didn't tell the Captain how we spent our break, he wouldn't have done anything except tell us not to do it again, but why put him on the spot. The fire was out and we were back in quarters by 4 a.m. In the morning when I got home I showed my wife how to shot-gun a beer and talked her into trying it. After the first beer took her by surprise and spilled all over her, she was determined to try again. The next beer went down easily and we both had a good laugh. It's great when your wife is also your best friend.

As the weeks roll by we all take our turn riding the ambo, taking details, and doing all the things that make up our job description. We are the only city agency that cuts our own grass, cleans our windows, and cleans our own toilets. We pay for our television, our coffee maker and anything else we might want in the house. The refrigerator and the oven are paid for by the city. Thieves can be a big problem to us, not by the members but by the people we are trying to protect. During my stay at Engine 25 our television was stolen twice, as well as a pair of work shoes. The shoes were stolen while we were out on a run when someone gained entrance through an unlocked window. However, the thief was gracious enough to leave his shoes behind. It was not a very fair trade as far as the firefighter was concerned. His new black work shoes had been replaced by a pair of beat up purple tennis shoes with the backs smashed down.

When we went out the door for a run or any other reason, you had to make sure the house was locked up tight or there was a good chance thieves would make off with something. One legendary Engine 25 story that occurred before my time there happened while the company was out and a drunk came in and stole the second line fire engine that was stored in quarters. He actually got it started, opened the back doors and drove away in it. He was caught a few blocks away and when asked where he was going he replied "I'm going to the fire." Instead he was going to jail and the engine was taken back to quarters.

More and more of my off time is spent with the same people I work with. We all bowl on the same team in the fire department bowling league and we go to the bars together. Some of the best parties I've ever been to were not planned but were a result of impromptu get-togethers after bowling. Stan, Doug, Chuck, and numerous others would meet at the local pub to continue the drinking which had started about an hour before we even got started bowling. By the time the bar closed at 2 a.m., we had a large number of people who didn't want to quit partying. That's when the real party would start. Stan was a bachelor who had his own house and we would go over there and the party would continue all night. As long as I live I will never forget his address because it was given out to anybody who wanted to come. That's an address that will live on in infamy.

CHAPTER 12
People Trapped

Thursday, July 17, 1975 was a very quiet night for us at work. I had the 2 a.m. to 4 a.m. watch that night and we didn't go out the door one time during that stretch. I woke Bob Smalls up at 4:15 a.m. for the 4 to 6 a.m. watch and told him "it's been nice and quiet tonight, try to keep it that way." "I'll do the best I can," he said as he took his seat at the desk. I went to bed, hoping to get two hours of sleep but I didn't even get to close my eyes. Bang, the lights went on and the gong woke everybody up. We turned out as Bob was hollering, "Everybody goes, 536 Laurens Street, dwelling fire." The 500 block of Laurens Street was only 2½ blocks from us and we were going to be first in. Stan was riding the pipe and I was riding lead-off as we turned on to Laurens Street.

Stan had actually never really become fully awake on the short dash to Laurens Street and I had to holler to him to get ready, that we had a dwelling and it was really off. Flames were blowing out the windows and front door and people were out front screaming that there were children inside. I was dropped at the nearest hydrant, which was almost directly in front of the dwelling, and Stan masked up and grabbed the 1½ inch line and went to the front door. Flames were shooting out the door like a blowtorch as I hooked up to the hydrant and I knew that this was going to be a tough one to fight. I ran to the pumper, grabbed a mask and went to back up Mitch Johnson and Stan who was on the pipe as he fought his way in the front door. We only had air bottles that would last for a half hour under ideal conditions and this was far from ideal.

I could hear Stan sucking air as he moved down the hallway and I knew his air would not last more than 15 minutes. He was throwing water on the ceiling as he crawled but he might as well have been pissing on it for all the good it was doing. This place was really off and the heat was tremendous, making it hard to catch your breath even with a mask on. Stan's bell went off letting him know he was almost out of air and I moved up to take the pipe. I knew I had more air than he did because I had not been in there as long as he had, nor had I taken the amount of heat he had taken. I grabbed the pipe and continued to move forward until I came to a set of narrow steps that led to the second and third floors. As I moved into the stairway, the blast of heat that hit me almost sucked the oxygen right out of me. There was fire as far as I could see in the stairway and I felt like I was going to melt right into the stairs. I had the pipe wide open and started up the stairs on my knees trying to stay as low as I could possibly stay. I felt like I was trying to crawl up a chimney.

I made it to the second floor landing and turned on to the third floor steps and started up. If anything, this was worse than the previous floor. I knew I was sucking down air at a tremendous rate but there was nothing I could do about it. As I neared the third floor landing, I could hear my warning bell going off but I decided to ignore it, thinking I don't have much further to go and I should have enough oxygen to last me. As I got to the top of the steps and hit the fire in the nearest room to me, my mask sucked into my face and I was out of air. I ripped my mask off and the heat and smoke was too much for my lungs. I turned and dove for the steps and tried to make my way back down but some of the steps had burned away and I fell through them about 10 feet. I landed on my back and scrambled to my feet and made my way outside.

As I walked over to the step of Truck 4, I saw Stan and a firefighter from Truck 11 sitting there nursing injuries. An ambo was on the scene and transported us all to Mercy Hospital. It was not until we were in the hospital that we found out just how bad it really was.

The final total was six killed and eight injured. Killed in the fire was Johnlene Gwynn - 18, Rochelle Gwynn - 15, John Gywnn - 12, April Gwynn - 5, Edward Gwynn - 2, and Laverne Nelson - 18[2]. To make matters worse, the fire was started intentionally by a man named Anthony Blackwell, because Johnlene owed him 20 dollars[3]. I found out later that I had crawled right over top of the 2 year old on the steps without knowing it. He was burned right into the steps and his body was not discovered until after the fire was out.

I found out that the reason the heat was so terrific in the stairway was because the plaster walls had been replaced with sheets of tin by the landlord all the way up to the third floor. I was treated for smoke inhalation, as was Stan Williams. The firefighter from Truck 11 was treated for a laceration of the nose and eyelid and a firefighter from Engine 1 was treated for first and second degree burns on his arm. There were many brave attempts to rescue the occupants, not the least of which involved a firefighter from Truck 4 and Chris Foster from Engine 13. They found a girl on the second floor under a pile of burning bedding and debris. They carried the badly burned girl outside and performed mouth-to-mouth and closed chest massage, but it was too late. Anthony Blackwell, 19 years old, was arrested one block away and was charged with murder. He had been arguing with Johnlene about $20 and told her he would burn her out if she didn't give him the money. He was found guilty and sentenced to death but it was overturned and changed to life in prison. He would be eligible for parole in 20 years by which time he would be 39. The Maryland judicial system turns my stomach.

---

2 Jennings, J. and William Lally. (1975, July 17). Arson Blamed, Suspect Held. *The Baltimore Sun.*

3 Hiltner. G. (1976, March 10). Blackwell Guilty, Faces Death in Arson-Murders. *The Baltimore Sun, pp A1*

CHAPTER 13
High Rises

Of all the places that we respond to, the high rises are my least favorite. We have four that we go to on almost a daily basis. 851 George St., 720 George St., 1058 Argyle Ave., and 900 Argyle Ave. All of these buildings smell exactly the same; a combination of piss, grease, garbage, and shit. That is the only way I know to describe the smell and I don't think that does it justice. We are constantly in one of these buildings for a variety of reasons; trash chute on fire, apartment on fire, pot of food, mattress fires, and false alarms. The elevators very seldom work, the stand pipes have all been vandalized and there is always the chance that you will be hit by something thrown from the upper floors.

When we go for the trash chute on fire, which we do almost every Sunday, the Engine company goes to the highest floor that the trash is burning on. We take a metal box with all the necessary attachments we need to hook up to the stand pipe. After almost rebuilding the stand pipe, we take a line, stick it in the chute and open it up full blast for about 5 to 10 minutes. The water runs all the way down to the trash compactor on the first floor where the truck men are pulling the stuck garbage apart with ceiling hooks. Of course they have to chase the rats away before they go in the room, no easy job considering that some of the rats are the size of small dogs. When the water makes its way down and finally saturates the garbage enough, we put up and go home, only to be called to another high rise later in the day.

An apartment fire in a high rise is another animal all together. If we are lucky, one of the elevators is working and we take that to the floor below the fire. If we know for sure that we have a good fire, the ride up in the elevator is usually relatively quiet. The only sounds are the hissing of the air bottles being turned on, the clank of equipment, helmets being adjusted and gloves checked. We didn't use air bottles in all fires but in high rise fires they were a necessity because of the lack of ventilation. We all have a job to do and our thoughts are on what we expect to find when we get up there. When the doors open, we are on the floor below the fire floor where we have to put the stand pipe together and make our way up the stairs.

All of the buildings are laid out the same, a large door at each end of a long hallway with apartments on both sides of the hallway. We mask up and open the door to start our way down the hall. The hallway is totally black with smoke. You cannot see your hand in front of your face. You stay low, either crawling on your belly or duck walking, and everything is done by feel. If you got a good look from the outside, you at least know which side of the hallway it is on and approximately how far down it is. The truck men are crawling with us, feeling the doors for heat until they find the one that is burning. If we are lucky the door is open; if not, the truck men have to beat it open with a maul. We crawl in and find the fire with no trouble. All the apartments are small and made of concrete which holds the heat in like an oven. There are no ceilings to pull or walls to open. The only thing that can burn is the furniture and the residents. The truck men open the windows and the patio door to ventilate and make a search of the rooms. We throw everything that burned off the balcony, scoop out the water with the shovels, roll the hose up and get out.

I always checked my clothes when we got back to make sure I had not picked up any hitchhikers. How anybody can live in that filth is beyond me and almost all of it is self-induced. It's the people that live there that make it the stinking rat hole that it is. Drug dealings, shootings, and stabbings are commonplace and I pity the decent people that have to live there. I'd rather live on the street.

We were on the elevator one day when we noticed something dripping from the ceiling. When we investigated, we found a body on the roof of the elevator. His blood was dripping through the ceiling and onto the floor from his numerous stab wounds. Needless to say, he was dead as a doornail so we called the police and let them figure it out. If I never went down there again it wouldn't bother me.

The other night I was on the ambo and we responded to a house in the 1200 block of Myrtle Ave. I got out of the ambo and walked up to the front door but as I turned the knob, the door was pulled open from the inside. A woman shoved an infant into my arms and ran outside screaming hysterically. I looked down at the unconscious baby and it was immediately apparent that he was terribly burned. I ran to the ambo and placed him on the stretcher and climbed in after him. We rushed him to Maryland General Hospital but it was too late. He was dead on arrival. I was wearing a long sleeve uniform shirt and when I looked down at my arms all I could see was the skin from the baby stuck to my shirt. The father came rushing into the hospital only to be told that his son was dead. He ran back outside cursing that he was going to kill the person responsible for the death of his son. It turned out that a friend of the family, who was babysitting, got tired of the baby crying and put him in a tub of boiling water to shut him up.

The next morning when I got home I did the same thing I had done many times before after a particularly hard night. I walked in and looked at my boys sleeping in their beds and couldn't take my eyes off them. The difference in where I work and where I'm raising my boys is like another solar system. I don't know how much longer I can continue to ride this ambo. The cruelty to children that I witness is overwhelming.

On December 13th, my birthday, we are on day work when we hear a box come in for a fire in a nursing home in the 1200 block of Fayette Street. It is just up the street from Truck 13, one of the best Truck Companies in the city that sits by itself on Carey St. It does not take long for a second alarm to be struck out and I am on my way. I'm driving Battalion Chief 4 and it doesn't take long to get there. When we pull up, firefighters are rescuing people everywhere you look. A third alarm has been requested and the main thing on my mind is how many people are going to die today. We take the rear of the building and heavy smoke is pouring out of the building.

Residents are being assisted down ladders and carried out the back door and I am amazed at the job that is unfolding in front of me. There is no yelling or very many orders being given, just dedicated firefighters doing one hell of a job. When the fire was finally brought under control, almost an hour later, we realize how good a job was really done at this fire. There are no fatalities and only two patients are hospitalized; both with chest pains and they are expected to be released the next day. What a great job by everyone involved!

Less than a month later, on January 3, 1976, we are again on day work when a box is struck out for the same place. Lincoln Convalescent Center, 1200 block of Fayette Street is on fire again. I'm riding Engine 13 and we take it on the third alarm. The fourth floor is off and rolling but we are lucky this time. Although there are no residents on the fourth floor, everyone has to be evacuated from the building anyway. Four alarms are needed to accomplish both jobs, fight the fire and help the residents out of the building. There is obviously a fire bug on the loose and I hope they catch him before he kills somebody.

Most of the major fires are really spectacular to look at but relatively easy to fight. Once you get there and find out what you have to do and get set up the rest is usually surround and drown. The best thing about the big fires is it gives you the chance to renew old acquaintances. I would walk around when the opportunity arose and look up guys that I had not seen since fire school or guys that I used to work with. We would shake hands and ask about the family, compare this fire with the last big one we were on and make arrangements to meet up at a later date. It was almost like a family reunion.

CHAPTER 14
Screw Ups

In between major fires is when the real work took place; the one and two alarm fires, where all the work was inside out of the view of the public eye. Of course some things happen that you are glad the public can't see. I had an experience one night when I was still a rookie that I was glad the civilians didn't see. We were first in on a dwelling fire on Division Street and when we pulled up, it didn't look like it was going to be too tough. From the looks of the smoke I figured it to be a bedroom fire and it was. I was riding the pipe and we advanced the line up the steps to the second floor. When we got to the top of the steps, I looked to my right and I could see the fire in the rear bedroom. I turned toward it and opened the pipe. I expected to darken it down quickly and take another look at it but the water didn't seem to be having any effect on the fire. I crawled a few feet closer and opened the pipe again but once again the fire stayed burning. In fact, it seemed to be intensifying. I suddenly felt more and more heat on the back of my neck. I looked over my shoulder and there is a fire raging away in the front bedroom. I turned around and crawled back the way I had come and hit it with a good shot. The fire quickly died down and we were able to finish it off but I still didn't know about the other bedroom fire. As the smoke lifted, I could see why I was not having any effect on the back bedroom fire. There was no room at that end of the hallway. There was a big mirror that was reflecting the front room fire back at me and I had hit it with enough water to put out a room twice that size. Everybody on the fire ground knew about it before I got outside to take a break. Needless to say I was the butt of quite a few jokes for a while. I would have to wait for someone else to screw up to take the heat off of me. It would not take long.

We had a good fire going on Calhoun Street near Engine 8 and Truck 10. The fill-in driver for Engine 8 went the wrong way and somehow ended up facing Truck 10 in front of the fire building. He then proceeded to take his lead off line and put it into the intake valve for the deck gun instead of the intake for the pumps. When he got water from the hydrant, it went right to the deck gun which was pointing right at Truck 10. It almost blew the windshield right out of the truck. Captain Brinkman, the truck captain, was screaming at him to shut it down but there was no closing valve for the deck gun, it was a straight shot right from the hydrant to the front of the truck. After the fire was out, we all had a good laugh about it except the pipe man from Engine 8 who had been inside the whole time waiting for water. He said he felt like a rack of ribs on the grill as he waited in vain for water. To make matters worse, Engine 25 instead of Engine 8 put the fire out which is worse than getting beat in by another company. It put my mirror episode on the back burner and for that I was thankful.

It is now 1976 and I am enjoying watching my boys grow up. Ray is six now and on the wild side and I think he is going to be a load in the future. Steve is much quieter but is fearless when it comes to his own safety. Ray is in little league and seems to enjoy the competition. He is a good athlete who likes to take charge when he is on the field. He plays almost every position in the field at one time or another and hits the ball hard when at bat. But it is Steve who seems to be a natural. The first time I gave him a ball and told him to throw it to me, he turned sideways and threw with a natural motion. I don't know for sure but I think that is unusual for such a young age. Lois is teaching them all the right manners that I was never really very good at doing. I love being a father, maybe because I never knew mine. We have a good family atmosphere at home and most of the credit goes to Lois. She just seems to know what to say and when to say it.

On February 17, 1976, we are working night shift at Engine 13 and the card game is in full swing. At 7:52 p.m., a box is struck out for a building fire at 106-108 Hopkins Place downtown near the Civic Center. Bob Smalls is on watch and listening to the radio and hollers back to the kitchen that it sounds like a good one. We break up the card game and walk up to the watch desk to listen with him. Someone pulls the run card to see where we stand if they pull a second alarm. We take it on the third if it goes that far. Suddenly we hear Battalion Chief 5 say "give me a fifth alarm." He has skipped the second, third, and fourth alarms and went right to the fifth! Within seconds Engine 13 and Truck 4 along with the Chief are on their way. I am thinking to myself, "there are going to be a lot of companies on the street at the same time all going to the same location." I know the fill-in pump operator is aware of this too and will be on the lookout for other companies.

We are screaming down Martin Luther King Blvd. approaching Fayette Street and there is a cop directing traffic on the corner. I'm looking over the pump operator's shoulder at the cop and I see he is signaling frantically in both directions, when he suddenly runs to the curb. At almost the same time, I see Truck 13 come flying down Fayette Street right at us. "Watch out!" I scream as the pump operator jerks the wheel to the left and we watch as Truck 13 makes a hard right on to M.L.K. and misses us by a few feet. We don't even slow down but we all know how close it was.

As we turn onto Hopkins Place, I can't believe what I'm looking at. We have a six story building and it is fully involved, top to bottom, all the floors are burning. It doesn't seem possible that a six story building can become that involved that quickly but I'm looking at it and it is. Flames are shooting 100 feet in the air above the top of the building and are starting to lick across the narrow alley into the old B&O building on Lombard Street. Companies are setting up water curtains trying to stop the fire from jumping to the other building.

We are sent inside the B&O building to look for any extension of the fire. We go up to the fifth floor and look inside a bathroom and sure enough the flames from next door have eaten their way through the wooden shutters and

View of 106-108 Hopkins Place. (The Baltimore Sun)

started a fire in the ceiling. We knock it down quickly and go to the next room; same thing there, small amount of fire that we knock down quickly. We hit three rooms and didn't find anything else so we had a bird's eye view of the fire from then on. Later we find out that Rescue 1 was briefly trapped and had to be rescued from the fire escape on the fifth floor. Within 39 minutes there are a total of nine alarms struck out bringing 250 firefighters to the scene.

The fire could be seen from all over the city and hundreds of people gathered to watch it. There was a hockey game that night at the Civic Center scheduled for 8 o'clock and all the people that were there for that were also watching. The original fire building eventually collapsed into a giant pile of rubble but it didn't spread any further. We had had high winds most of the day but the wind had died down about 6 p.m. If they hadn't, who knows what would have happened? Everyone involved suspected arson but as usual there was not enough proof and no charges were ever brought. It was a spectacular fire to witness but we were glad when we were finally released and could go back to Engine 13.

CHAPTER 15
Never a Dull Moment

A few weeks later I'm sitting on watch on day work when a man runs in with an infant in his arms. "I don't know what's wrong," he says. "He's not breathing." I take the baby from him and check his pulse and get nothing. I throw the gong and lay the baby on the watch desk. I start mouth to mouth as the rest of the guys come rushing up to see what's going on. The ambo is out as usual and we call for one and continue to work on the baby but we are getting no response. We also ask for the police, the man that brought the baby in does not seem too concerned, and that is upsetting. The ambo arrives and takes the baby away but we don't hold out much hope. Later in the day when our ambo returns, we find out that the baby was shaken to death by the guy that brought him to the firehouse. He was arrested and is in jail. I hope if he is found guilty, they put him in the general prison population. He wouldn't last a week.

On June 1st, I am detailed to Rescue 1 at the Super House. Riding Rescue 1 does not mean that I know what I'm doing. I am just a body that will do what the officer tells me to do. If it is similar to truck work, I'll be okay but if it involves the jaws-of-life or the huge air bag or any other special equipment that they have, I'm out of my league. I've never been trained on any of that equipment.

We are in quarters early in the evening watching the news, our fellow fire-fighters are demonstrating against City Hall at the temporary location off of Baltimore Street. City Hall itself was undergoing renovations. We are getting screwed again in our contract negotiations and the men are fed up. Our TV watching is interrupted by the watch-desk tones and the speaker alerting us to a building fire at 200 East Baltimore Street, not far from the demonstration. We weave through the streets of downtown Baltimore and we can see the smoke from blocks away. As we pull up in front, the flames are leaping from the third floor of the Trademark Restaurant. There is a large bay window on the third floor and it explodes with flame as we arrive. Truck 2 is on the scene and their aerial ladder is going to the roof as I exit the rescue wagon. I am going to help throw ground ladders when I notice that no one is going up the aerial ladder. I grab an axe and look again and still there is no one on the aerial ladder so I decide that I will go up to ventilate the roof. When I get to the roof, I can see that there is a large scuttle on the roof of the fire building and it is still intact. It must be 6 feet by 6 feet and the smoke is puffing out around the edges. I'm a little leery, truck work is not something I'm used to and I know the floor under me is fully involved. But I know the roof has to be opened up for the guys inside. I'm used to being the guy inside and I know how much of a difference it makes. I pry the edge of the scuttle up and the whole thing blows off with a tremendous roar scaring me half to death. I leap backwards and watch as a square column of smoke blasts out and up into the sky. "Man," I say to myself, "that son of bitch is ventilated now." I make my way over to the fire escape and go down one floor at a time smashing out the back windows and watching the smoke come rolling out. By the time I get down on the ground and around front, the engine companies have put a good stop on it. I make my way up the inside stairs and start to help with the pulling of ceilings checking for extension. As we start to overhaul, I'm talking to one of the engine men and he tells me that when the roof got opened, the smoke must have lifted four feet and the heat became much more bearable. I don't tell him it was me that opened the roof but I feel pretty good about it.

There is a lot more to putting these fires out than just throwing water on them. I was on the other side on this fire and I liked it. I'm glad we did a good job on this fire because we had quite an audience, 600 firefighters had been watching the whole thing from across the street. It seems like no matter how the city treats us, the job still gets done. I guess the powers that be know this and take advantage of us at contract time. It's a damn shame.

We clear the fire ground and go back to the super house but not for long. A violent thunderstorm is rolling across the city and we don't expect to be in quarters for very long; car accidents and/or another building fire is a good probability. At a little after 8 p.m. we are called out again, this time for a car with a tree on it in the 2200 block of Belair Road. I know just where this is, not far from where I live, and the trees in that block are huge. We hear Engine 19 on the scene and they tell dispatch to let the rescue come on in, they have a bad accident.

We get there and I am amazed at the scene that is in front of me. A huge tree has fallen across Belair Road and landed right on top of a Cadillac with four people inside as they were driving down the street. The roof of the car is crushed onto the front seat and I don't see how anyone can be alive in that car. We are told that the two people in the back seat have already climbed out and are not injured but not a sound has been heard from the front seat. I climb onto the back of the car and go in the rear window onto the back seat. There's not much room to work as I make my way towards the front of the car. I move forward and get my head in between the front seats and look at the driver first. I have to look away and look back to make sure I'm seeing what I think I'm seeing. The tree has fallen on the top front of his face and had torn his face completely off. All his skin is lying in his lap and I'm looking at his skull with just a thin sheen of blood on it. I quickly look at the passenger and I can see that it is a female and she is also obviously dead. The tree has missed her face but has crushed her chest and torn her breasts off. I don't think they ever knew what hit them, I hope not anyway.

It takes a long time to extricate them both, the tree has to be sawed up and the roof has to be cut off. We cover them with blankets when we pull them out to spare the crowd and to give the victims a little dignity. They are later identified as 52 year old Paul Brice and his neighbor Viola Curtis who is also in her 50's[4]. They were in the wrong place at the wrong time and fate was not on their side. We later found out the storm packed winds over 60 miles per hour and had blown down over 30 trees, shattered a large glass window at Johns Hopkins Hospital, and tore a roof off a house on Fort Avenue. We don't get back to quarters until nearly midnight and the rest of the night is quiet. I won't have nightmares about what I saw but I'm sure I'll never forget it. It was a hell of a night.

The next shift, I'm back at Engine 13 and its day work so I'm back into the same routine. Beds have to be made, toilets cleaned, sinks cleaned, floors waxed and so on and so on. I like night work better, more fires, no house work, and I don't have to listen to the alarm clock at home screaming at me at 5 a.m. The neighborhood where I live is a middle class, blue collar neighborhood in Northeast Baltimore. I would like to move and raise my kids in a nicer place but it is not to be for awhile. But where I live is a lot better than where I work.

4 (1976, June 2). Thunderstorm Lashes Area, Kills Two. *The Baltimore Sun, pp D1*

CHAPTER 16
The Neighborhood

Even though I've worked in the same neighborhood for four years now, I still can't get over how filthy and crime ridden it is. James Schuster told me that in the fifties and early sixties it was a nice neighborhood. Pennsylvania Avenue was the place to be if you wanted to see some of the great black musicians and singers of their time. But now the drugs and the broken families have taken their toll. All the night clubs have closed and moved away and the buildings are vacant rat traps used by the junkies to shoot up in. Trash is discarded on the streets as if it belongs there, adding to the bleakness of the neighborhood. Junkies are walking around like zombies in a bad movie looking for their next fix. Children are out at all hours of the night without any parents around and as a result, they more or less control the streets after dark. They do whatever they want to the decent people in the neighborhood with no fear of the police. The poor people that are trapped in this neighborhood and can't afford to flee are like prisoners in their own homes after darkness sets in. There are rats as big as cats everywhere you look and dogs wandering around that are skin and bones. When I get to work I feel as if I'm in a third world country and I am always glad to get home, which compared to where I work, feels like Shangri-La.

Engine 13 sits on the Southeast edge of this neighborhood on the corner of McCulloh Street and McMechen Street. We are almost on an island. There are no residential houses behind us or to the left of us, only the three story row houses across the street on McCulloh Street. Our doors face North onto McMechen Street and there is a school across the street from us. It is ironic that if we come out of quarters and make a right, we only have to go three blocks and we are in a very exclusive neighborhood. In 1976, $200,000 row homes in Bolton Hill are not uncommon and the streets are always immaculate. Needless to say, we don't make very many right turns coming out of the station. A left turn takes us toward Engine 8 and Truck 10 and also towards Pennsylvania Avenue. Most of our runs and fires are in that direction or North towards my old Company, Engine 25. We have Engine 7 to our South and Engine 1 and Truck 11 to our East. When a box is struck out for a dwelling fire or building fire, we will be running with some of these companies or all of them, depending on where it is.

One alarm consists of four engines, two trucks and a chief. We have cards in a box on the watch desk that tell us which way to go to get to each box. All the drivers know the right route to take but if another company is in our quarters and they are not familiar with our district, they will use the cards to help them get to where they are supposed to be. The cards are also helpful to the rookies to learn where each box is located. At Engine 25 we were right next to the houses and we got to know the people that lived around us, for better or worse. At Engine 13 we don't have that and I can't say that I miss it; it's much quieter at night.

Parking has always been a problem no matter which house I was working in. At Engine 25 we parked on Gold Street, right next to the firehouse, and there was always a chance that your car would be broken into while we were out on a fire. One afternoon we heard a loud crash outside and we knew someone had run into one of our cars. We ran outside just in time to see two men running from their stolen car which was rammed into the side of my car. I was so mad I started to chase them down Tiffany Alley behind the firehouse. I chased them for three blocks and kept up with them as they turned right and passed Druid Hill Avenue. Just before they got to Pennsylvania Avenue, I realized that I was like the proverbial dog that chases cars; what is he going to do when he catches it? I was obviously the wrong color to be chasing two black guys in West Baltimore so I gave up and walked back to the firehouse. When I got back Willie asked me if I had lost my mind. I guess it was temporary insanity.

At Engine 13, we had a parking lot behind the house but it was not fenced in so the cars were like a smorgasbord to the thieves. Eventually it got so bad we just left the cars unlocked with nothing of value in them and hoped the thieves would not break the windows before they realized it was not locked. We had a cop on stakeout in the firehouse for a while but he never caught anybody. We also asked the powers that be to put a fence around the lot but as usual, our requests fell on deaf ears. One morning I came out after night work to find a cinder block through my windshield. I guess the thieves were not happy about finding nothing to steal. What irritated me was that the same guys that were doing all this were also the same guys that we would be saving on the street from drug overdoses or pulling out of a vacant dwelling fire. With all that said, I still would not want to be anywhere else. This is where the action is and you just have to take the good with the bad.

False alarms were also a constant problem. You could almost set your watch by some boxes. Box 367, Myrtle and Hoffman, would come in everyday when school let out. When we would pull up, there would be a crowd of kids standing on the corner next to the box. We would just get out and rewind the box and leave. There was no use asking if anybody saw anything. Of course they all knew who did it but to them it was just another form of entertainment. We did catch a guy once who was walking along at 3 a.m. pulling each box he came upon. It was easy to figure out which box was next after the first three false alarms and we were lying in wait. We watched him pull the box and we leaped out and ran him down. There were no police around and we decided to put the fear of God in him. Truck 4 raised their aerial ladder and we got the rope off the truck and put it over the top rung. We told him that pulling false alarms was a hanging offense and that was going to be his fate. He looked around to see if there were any cops around to help him and when he didn't see any he really got scared. We had two companies there and it really looked like we were serious but we were actually trying not to laugh. When the police got there, he was very grateful to see them and could not wait to be locked up. We laughed all the way back to quarters. Sometimes this job just cracks me up.

On June 28, 1976, we relieved the day shift on the fire ground at Dryden Oil Company off of North Avenue. This was one of the most spectacular fires ever seen in Baltimore. There were 11 alarms pulled before all was said and done and they needed every one of them. The thick black smoke rose 1,000 feet in the air and could be seen all the way in Towson, 15 miles away. There were 55 gallon oil drums shooting 100 feet in the air when they exploded and they sounded like cannons going off. There was also a shortage of hydrants so relays of pumpers had to be set up for over a quarter mile to get enough water on the fire. This was the third fire since April at Dryden and they were all arson, but this was by far the worst. We missed all this because the fire came in around noon. When we got there at 5 p.m., it was still burning but the worst was over. It was obviously another surround and drown but the guys from day shift said they had never seen anything like it. We were there most of the night and of course had to put all their hose away and clean up. Dryden Oil moved out of Baltimore after that and relocated to Baltimore County. I wish we had been there for the best part but there will always be more fires to fight in Baltimore.

Not long after the Dryden fire, we were on night work and went out for smoke in the area of the 1500 block of Myrtle Ave. We arrived on the scene and there was nothing visible but we could smell a mattress burning somewhere. We walked around the block without finding anything and the Captain sent the other companies home as we continued to search. We looked for another 20 minutes and still found nothing, but the smell of a mattress was still very strong and we hated to give up. Just as we were ready to call it quits, I saw a trace of smoke in the haze of the streetlight. I called the Captain over to look at it; we still could not figure out where it was coming from but it was definitely there. We all gathered around and looked at it from different angles and finally Stan Williams figured out that it was coming from the second floor of a dwelling in the middle of the block.

We got a line off the engine and went up the stairs and now you could really smell it. We kicked in the door and went down the hallway to the bedroom and sure enough there it was. It was a mattress and box springs burning and lying on top of it was an unconscious man with serious burns on his arm and leg. We rolled him off the mattress and put the fire out and called the ambo. I doubt that he ever knew how lucky he really was that we had stayed on the scene for over half an hour until we found the fire. It turned out he was so drunk he didn't even know he was on fire and he gave the ambo crew a hard time on the way to the hospital. Our clientele never cease to amaze me.

CHAPTER 17
Change

It seems as if the city fathers and the firefighters union have been at odds forever. We don't ask for much and still they give us less and less. The last contract called for half of one percent increase in wages for each of the two years the contract was in effect. They must be joking, but we don't have any recourse. We can't strike and they know it. Our "union" is like a paper tiger, it has no teeth. We can complain and bitch about it but in the end we have to take what they offer us. It's very frustrating to all of us because we feel as if we do the most dangerous work, with the best results, of any city agency. Every day and every night, somewhere in Baltimore, a firefighter is putting his life on the line protecting someone's property or saving someone's life and all we want in return is a livable wage, but Mayor Schaffer continues to low- ball us at contract time. I wonder if he has any idea how much he is hurting the most loyal employees he has. My guess is he does not care.

During 1976, Captain Graleski was promoted to Chief and our new Captain is Dave Zimmer. He was the captain of Truck 4 in our house but he decided to move over to the engine when he had the chance. We are not sure what to expect from him. He had a reputation on A-shift of being a hard disciplinarian, but then again A-shift was a tough shift to handle. We will just have to wait and see.

My first fire with our new Captain goes really well and I think he is really going to fit in. We pulled up to a dwelling fire on the corner of Druid Hill and Whitelock Street and the smoke was belching out of the basement. Battalion Chief 4, Chief Downing, who was a good chief but was very excitable on the fire ground, was already on the scene. To those of us who had been working with him, his excitability was nothing new but to anyone else it could be disturbing. As we exited the engine, Captain Zimmer looked over just in time to see the Chief disappear into the smoke filled cellar window without a line backing him up. "What the hell is he doing?" he asked me. "Ahh that's just him," I replied. "He does stuff like that all the time." "Well, get a line in there and help him out." I grabbed the booster line and made my way over to the window and climbed in. Sure enough, there he was lying on the floor eating smoke, waiting for me. "It's up front," he said as he coughed up a lung. I went on by him and proceeded to hit the fire as he made his way back out the window. Captain Zimmer came up behind me and we put the fire out without any problem but he was still scratching his head over the Chief's actions. "Does he do that all the time?" he asked. I laughed and told him that it was not unusual but we were used to it.

Chief Downing was a hands-on Chief and felt he had to make sure his orders were being carried out. One time we were at a high rise for smells and bells. We were all on the first floor when he told Truck 11 to go the third floor and check it out. Truck 11 got on the elevator and took it to the third floor and when the doors opened, there was Chief Downing standing there. He had taken the stairs and beat them up there! He was always the topic of conversation back in quarters but he was a good chief who knew his stuff. He was just a little excitable at times, but he was never a screamer.

To me, screamers are the worst kind of officer. They get everybody overly excited without accomplishing anything. Screaming at someone to ventilate the second floor does not make it happen any quicker than if you keep your cool and just give the order. I once had an officer following me down the stairs into the basement of the library building at the University of Baltimore. He was screaming all the way down. I knew that once we made the turn at the last landing it was going to get extremely hot, so I stopped just before the turn and pulled the flaps on my helmet down and pulled my collar up. The whole time he was screaming at me to keep going and why was I stopping. I was thinking to myself, "I know he's not going to be ready for this heat when we make this turn." Sure enough, we made the turn and I could hear him behind me, "Jesus Christ it's hot," and he had to go back around the corner and button up. If he hadn't wasted so much time screaming he would have realized that it was going to get very hot and he could have buttoned up ahead of time. I was smiling to myself as I moved further into the building.

Captain Zimmer wasn't excitable or a screamer. He used to walk around the firehouse practicing saying "working fire" all the time. When we asked him what he was doing he said he wanted it to sound just right on the radio when we were first in and he had to report a working fire. He even put a tape recorder next to the scanner on the table next to his bed. He said he was going to turn it on when he was turning out to listen to himself when he got back. Invariably he would forget to do it and would be kicking himself on the way to the fire. One night we turned out for box 3229, Lafayette and Druid Hill. I was driving and as soon as he got in the pumper he told me that he had turned the recorder on as he was turning out. We were first in but when we pulled up to the box there was nothing in sight and it looked like another false alarm. As he picked up the microphone to call it in, I looked over and saw flames rolling out the back window of a dwelling on McCulloh Street. "Look, there it is," I said as I made the left turn on to Lafayette. Here's his chance, I thought as he reached for the microphone again. He picked it up and proudly said, "We've got one." "You blew it," I said as we rounded the corner and pulled up out front. As we were putting the line in service I was laughing as I kept telling him he missed his chance. When we got back to quarters we all gathered around the tape recorder and listened to him say, "we've got one." We were laughing and he was laughing right along with us. He would have plenty of opportunities to get it right and he eventually did.

Captain Zimmer didn't mind pulling Chief Downing's string once in a while when the opportunity presented itself. At one time, Chief Downing was wearing a neck collar and a heart monitoring device at the same time. He seemed to have a myriad of problems sometimes. The Chief was downtown dropping off reports one day when we got a report of a dwelling fire on Calhoun Street. I was driving and the Captain was in the front seat with me. When we turned onto Calhoun Street all you could see was smoke coming from as many as five different two story dwellings. Captain Zimmer called in heavy smoke showing and then before he got out, he grabbed the microphone again and said, "we have smoke from five different dwellings and I'll give you an update later." Then he looked at me and said, "that ought to get him going," and laughed as he went to help with the line. We talked to the Chief's driver later that day to see how Chief Downing had reacted. He said that when the Captain called in heavy smoke the Chief started to remove the heart monitor but when he called in smoke from five dwellings, all he could hear was the sound of the neck collar being ripped off. It turned out that the fire was only in one dwelling but the smoke was traveling through a common cockloft and made it look worse than it was. It was another good Chief Downing story to be told around the card table at night.

On August 12, 1976, we had been on night work for less than an hour when a box was struck out for a building fire down in the Curtis Bay area. This was a long way from us, far south and near the water, a largely industrial area with a few small communities wedged in among warehouses and factories. The weather was extremely hot, over 90 degrees, not the kind of day to be fighting fires. We listened as the first companies on the scene called in a working fire and within three minutes a second and a third alarm had been pulled. We quickly pulled the card to see when we would go as they were pulling the fourth and the fifth alarms. We would take it on the seventh if it went that far and it sounded as if it would. Not long afterwards we were on our way, weaving in and out of traffic as we made our way down Hanover Street and crossed the Hanover Street Bridge into Cherry Hill. As we approached the intersection of Reedbird and Hanover, we could see that there had been an accident involving a pumper and a car. We stopped to see if they needed any assistance but were told there were no injuries so we continued on our way. When we got to the scene at the Empire Industrial Park at Curtis and Benhil, the smoke was hundreds of feet in the air. Flames and smoke were pouring from a two story metal building that was at least 400 feet deep and the fire was threatening to spread to the Alexandria Sheet Metal Corporation. An eighth alarm had been struck out by this time and it looked like it was going to be a long hot evening. We took our 2½ inch line on to the roof of an adjoining building and poured water onto the fire for hours. It was a very stubborn fire with extremely hot conditions. About halfway through the fire, Bob Smalls fainted from heat exhaustion. He was taken to the hospital and given fluids and placed off duty. He would return the next shift we worked to take the harassment from us he so richly deserved. The old saying is if you are looking for sympathy, do not look in a firehouse or a bar. We didn't let on how worried we really were when it first happened, as that would have ruined our fun.

We were on day work the following Sunday and instead of our usual slow day work, we were pretty busy. We went out to the 500 block of Laurens Street, and had light smoke showing. It turned out to be a mattress fire, which we handled along with Truck 4. If there is such a thing as a routine fire, this was it. We smelled it and knew what we had before we stopped the pumper. Grab the line, up the stairs, crawl down the hallway, into the bedroom, knock the worst of it down, help Truck 4 roll the mattress up and throw it out the window. We are on the scene less than 30 minutes. Two hours later, we are back in the 500 block of Laurens Street but a different house this time. Another mattress fire, second floor rear and we go about our job same as before. That's the first time I can remember that happening since I've been here. One hour later we are going back to the same block, different house, another mattress fire. This is unbelievable, three mattresses in occupied dwellings in one block in one day. There must have been a block party there last night or something. None of them were arson and nobody was hurt. It made the day go by very quickly and the next thing we knew we were in a local pub rinsing the smoke out of our mouths with a nice cold Bud. What a great country!

On November 2, we were on day work again when we were dispatched on a full box to 1600 Bolton Street for a report of a dwelling fire. We were first in and it didn't look like much as we got off the pumper. The dwelling was a three-story row house that had been undergoing renovation for some time. Bolton Street is in the exclusive neighborhood of Bolton Hill and we don't expect to have many fires there. The smoke that was showing was a wisp of smoke coming from under the windowsill on the side of the house. Charles Forte took a haligan bar and pried the windowsill off and we could see a little flame in the wall. We went inside and punched a hole in the wall and fire came leaping out at us. Now we knew we had a problem and we raced upstairs to check the wall above us. Another hole was punched and more fire came shooting out. Mitch Johnson, the first acting man who was in charge, asked for a second line to be brought in as the truck men proceeded to open the entire wall. The fire was racing throughout the house, in the walls, in the ceilings, and we couldn't seem to catch up with it. Before all was said and done, we had two alarms in and there was major damage to the first and second floor. It turned out that a painting crew was putting the finishing touches on a renovation project. They were burning the old paint off the windowsills and noticed some smoke coming from the sill. They got a garden hose and put water on it and forgot about it. Only when the smoke got heavier and heavier did they call the fire department. By then, the fire was raging inside the walls. At the height of the fire, the painters were seen loading their ladders and paint on their truck and pulling away. As we were fighting the fire the owner came home, saw what was going on, and broke down in tears. A $100,000 renovation down the tubes. Our day shifts have been pretty busy lately. I don't sit around wishing for someone's house to catch fire but if it happens and it's in our district that's all right with me.

CHAPTER 18
A Good Job

On November 4th, we are on night work and I'm detailed to Engine 18 on West 20th Street. It is a single house on a quiet residential street that still sees its share of fire service. They are sent across the Howard Street Bridge to our side of town to fight fires on a fairly regular basis. On this particular night, I hear Engine 13 go out on a box for a dwelling fire in the 1900 block of Etting Street. Etting Street is a very narrow street with small two story dwellings on each side of the street. Engine 18 only goes if there is a second alarm so I sat there and listened to the scanner. Engine 25 was first in and they reported heavy smoke showing from the second floor. It was not long until I heard the Chief call for a second alarm and off we went. We didn't do much; covered exposures in the house next door, and when it was over I went downstairs to see the guys in my company. I got the full story from them. The grandmother that lived there was babysitting and was on the first floor with a two year old asleep on the second floor when a neighborhood boy knocked on the door and told her that there was a fire on the second floor. She rushed up the stairs but was met by heavy smoke and fell down and barely got out of the house alive. When Engine 13 got to the front door, she was screaming that the baby was on the second floor in the middle room. Captain Zimmer rushed up the stairs, got down on his stomach and crawled into the middle room. The heat was too extreme to even attempt to stand up but he felt a crib as he crawled across the room. He reached out and tipped the crib over and the baby rolled out into his arms. He crawled back to the hallway just as the flames erupted over his head with the baby in his arms. He made it to the stairs and passed the baby down the steps to waiting firefighters. The little boy was rushed to the hospital and made a complete recovery. It was the third person Captain Zimmer had saved in the last few months and he was named firefighter of the year for 1976. The award could not have gone to a more deserving person. I hope he remembered to turn the recorder on.

Three nights later, we are working our last night of the shift and it has been relatively quiet. It is 2:54 a.m. when we are awakened by the gong and bunkroom lights. "Turn-out, 2015 Brunt Street, dwelling fire, everybody goes," Charles Forte hollers. Everybody is up and running for the apparatus in a matter of seconds. We pride ourselves on our ability to get out quick and tonight is no exception. Engine 25 is supposed to be first in but they are out on another call. That makes us first in and we don't have far to go. Brunt Street is a half block from Pennsylvania Avenue, a very small street much like Etting Street, where we had the fire our first night in. It is nothing but old two story row houses that burn like kindling. As we arrive on the scene, there is heavy smoke and flames coming from every window on the first and second floors and rolling out the front door. A woman is standing in the street screaming that her mother and daughter are inside, and looking at her face there can be no doubt she knows this to be true. There is absolutely no way for any of us to attempt a rescue, the house is fully involved and we have to beat the flames back starting at the front door. I take the inch and a half line off and start towards the front door. We have to go up about eight cement steps leading to the door and it is so hot we have to crawl up the outside steps to even get to the front door. We battle our way in knocking down the flames as we crawl across the living room and make our way to the back of the house. The house is not very deep and it does not take much to knock the bulk of the fire on the first floor. I can hear Engine 8 making their way up the stairs to the second floor and I know it won't be long before this fire is out. As the smoke starts to rise and we are able to see a few feet in front of us, we all see it at the same time. The grandmother is lying on the floor near the basement steps and she is burnt to a crisp. Her thighs have split open and there is only raw meat to look at. We make our way over to her and then we realize that the baby is underneath her and has been burnt so bad it looks like it is just one person instead of an adult and an infant. All we can do is wait for the coroner to take them away in a body bag. The fire started from a faulty space heater on the first floor and from the looks of things, they never had a chance. It is a bad night and we overhaul quietly.

I wore an air mask on this fire and I'm doing that more and more now that they are mounted in a bracket on the back of our jump seats. It is much better on my lungs but I feel like my visibility is less. Most of the time I decide whether or not to use one when we pull up to the fire. If it's a pot of food or a mattress fire, I usually don't wear one. The truck men seem to wear it most of the time and I can understand why. They do not have the hose to protect them and to give them that little air pocket I've come to depend on. They are constantly above the fire searching for people and I think it is easier for them to become disoriented. I know I should wear it more than I do and I'm going to make a conscious effort to do just that.

It is now December and the fire season is in full bloom. We never seem to go a shift without a good fire. Most are one alarm but we like to think that we did a good job on a lot of them to hold them to one alarm. On December 18th, we are listening to the radio as a fire is being fought in the 2900 block of Calvert Street. Heavy fire has been reported in a three story occupied dwelling and it is only a little after 6:00 in the morning. This could turn out to be a nasty one. Suddenly, we hear the Chief asking for more ambos for injured firefighters and he also asks for a second alarm. We don't go until the third alarm but we are getting ready. The Chief asks for a third and we are on our way. The houses in this block are very large three story row houses used mostly by students from Johns Hopkins University. I am driving and I hook up to a plug to pump in case it's needed. A fourth alarm has been transmitted but it does not look as if we will need it.

I find out later that as the men on the first alarm were going up the stairs, there was a flashover in the stairwell. A flashover is when superheated gases suddenly ignite and flash over everything in its path. It can be very deadly to firefighters. Firefighters Jeff Maynard and Albert Letts suffered first and second degree burns and firefighter Harold Mitchell cut his hand.[5] It could have been a lot worse. While this was going on, firefighters from Truck 16 had found three unconscious people on the third floor and the only way to get them down was by ladder. They had entered the building from a 35-foot ladder and it was going to be extremely hard to carry three unconscious people back down this ladder. Another 35-foot ladder was then thrown next to the original and the firefighters brought all three victims down working together off both ladders. It was a remarkable rescue and to make it even better all three victims were revived and lived to tell about it. All three were students in their early twenties.

Later, the father of one of the students visited the station of Truck 16 and thanked the men profusely for saving his daughter. He even offered them a reward but it was turned down with the explanation that saving them was enough of a reward. That may sound corny but it tells you something about the caliber of people I work with every day. It is a good fraternity to belong to.

[5] (1976, December 19). 3 Rescued from Blaze in Serious Condition. *The Baltimore Sun, pp A12*

CHAPTER 19
Off Duty

The men of Engine 13 and Truck 4 continue to get along and have good times both on duty and off. Stan Williams, Doug Falls [the talker], Charles Forte, Bryan Jones, a new addition to Truck 4 who transferred in after he realized how much fun we were having, and numerous other firefighters from around the city all bowl in the fire department bowling league. We all bowl duckpins, which in my opinion are much harder than 10 pins, and there are some really good bowlers in the league. The top 15 averages go to Washington each year to bowl against the D.C. firefighters for bragging rights and a trophy. I was lucky enough to make it this year and I had a great time. We won and it was the third time in a row that Baltimore had won so we got to retire the trophy.

I'm also playing on the fire department baseball team. We play a few colleges including the plebes at the naval academy. At the end of the season we play the police department team at Memorial Stadium before an Oriole game. Playing at the stadium is like my little league dream come true. There are some really good players on this team, most of them are better than me, but I do start in left field. We have a catcher named Bill Goodwin who is a really big guy with a lot of talent. At the stadium he hit a ball that never got higher than 15 feet that hit the right field wall, which was the opposite field for him. Tom McLhinney also hit the wall in left field with a line drive. My contribution was a walk after which I was promptly picked off first base, but we won and it was a lot of fun. I also recently went on a white-water rafting ride in West Virginia with a bunch of firefighters from different companies. It had been raining for about two weeks and the water was really high, therefore the guides recommended that we not go. When we told them we were all firefighters from Baltimore and we didn't care about how high the water was, they agreed to take us on the condition that they put two guides in each raft instead of one. We quickly agreed and pushed off for the wildest ride I've ever had on the water. The trip was supposed to last eight hours with a stop for lunch but we were going so fast that lunch was cancelled and we were done in four hours. There were six of us to a raft plus the two guides and we were thrown around like rag dolls. At one time I found myself in the air above the raft and I was sure I was going to land in the water but when I came down I landed right on top of Martin Ross and Andy Morris who were as surprised as I was. It was a great trip and it just added to the feeling of camaraderie among us even though we were from different companies.

CHAPTER 20
Death on the Fireground

The next year started out just like 1976 had left off, lots of fires and more rescues. On January 22nd, we had a good one-alarm fire in the 500 block of Calhoun Street. Four people were rescued by Truck 13 from the back porch of the dwelling and another three people were injured but lived to tell about it. We were last in and really didn't have much to do but it was a good job by Engine 8, Truck 10, and Truck 13. It never ceases to amaze me the number of fires that are fought and good jobs that are performed everyday by the firefighters in Baltimore City.

On March 4th, we were on night work when a box was struck out for a fire in the Fiberglass Specialties Company in the 5200 block of Fairlawn Avenue in Northwest Baltimore. Engine 46 was first in and we heard Captain Sappe call in that the building was fully involved. It was only six minutes later that a second alarm was struck out and we started to get ready. It was then that we heard someone on the radio screaming that they needed an ambo for an injured firefighter and it sounded real serious. In less than a minute the same person screams "where's the fucking ambo," over the air and we knew that it was a very serious situation. There was no need for a third alarm so we didn't go. We were left wondering who was hurt and how bad. It was not long until we found out. Captain Sappe, my rafting partner, had been killed when a 20-foot cinder block wall collapsed on him. Firefighter Bill Pohlman and the Captain were advancing a line in a garage door, hitting the flames when the Captain told firefighter Pohlman to shut the nozzle down and move to a different location. As he shut the hose down and started to move, they could hear something falling inside the building. Suddenly and without any warning, the cinder block wall next to them fell on Captain Sappe and caused massive head injuries. Pohlman, who was moving back at the time, escaped with leg injuries. When the roof of the one story building had collapsed it had caused the wall to buckle and this was what killed the Captain. Chief Kemp was in charge of the fire and when he was told that the Captain had died, he gathered everyone on the fire ground around him and told them. A lot of tears were shed that night. Captain Sappe was 34 years old and the father of three children. When word of his death reached us, it was met with stunned silence; it just did not seem possible that he was gone in an instant. Chief Curtis, the Chief of the fire department said, "Captain Sappe was a young, intelligent, dedicated officer, without a doubt this is one of the worst days in my entire career in the fire department."[6] I could not agree more.

---

6 Lally, W (1976, March 4) Blaze Kills fireman Here. *The Baltimore Sun.*

The death of Captain Sappe was a tragic event but of course it did not slow down the number of fires in Baltimore City. Day shift, night shift, A, B, or C-shift, the fires never stop. On March 6th, we have three alarms on Preston Street, one fatality, three buildings damaged. The one alarm fires are too numerous to count as the cold winter slowly gives way to warmer temperatures. On March 30th, we are on night work and so is an arsonist in Northwest Baltimore. The series of fires began around 10 p.m. when the rear door of the Danko-Arlington Co. at 4800 Wabash Ave. was set on fire. An hour later the rear door of the Car Care Center at 4805 was torched and he was just getting started. One and a half hours later two floors of the abandoned Hughes Lumber Company at 5003 Reisterstown Rd. are set on fire. We responded to this one and while we were there fighting it, another fire was set in a vacant building at 5028 Reisterstown Rd.

When we get back from the lumberyard fire, my clothes are soaking wet and my gloves are thoroughly soaked. I change clothes and put my gloves on the radiator to dry. It is 2:00 a.m. and I have to go on watch. I have the 2:00 to 4:00 a.m. watch tonight and I'm fighting sleep. At 3:22, I am looking out the watch desk window across the schoolyard and I suddenly see flames burst out of the windows in a house at 1700 Madison Avenue. I throw the gong and two companies of very tired firefighters turn out for the ninth time that night. We are first on the scene and this place is going good. As we are putting our line in service, Truck 4 throws a ladder to the second floor and brings a man down who immediately steps on broken glass which slices his feet wide open. The fire is on the third floor and Captain Zimmer and I make our way up the stairwell pulling the 1 1/2 inch line as we go. We get to the top of the stairs and I can tell that this is not just one room; every room is burning and I can hear the crackling of the flames as they eat their way across the ceilings. I have a mask on, as does the Captain, but when I reach for my gloves I realize that in my rush to turn out, I left them on the radiator. We are waiting for water and I can feel the heat bearing down on us so I turn to the Captain and tell him I don't have any gloves. I ask him if he has a pair and he says "yeah I've got some," and he pulls a pair from his turnout coat pocket. Then he smiles and says, "but they are the only pair I have," and he proceeds to put them on his hands. We get water and we start the long crawl down the hallway but my hands feel like they will burst into flames any minute. I finally put them in my turnout coat and put the pipe under my arm and keep going. I can't aim the nozzle as well as I would like but I'm getting the job done.

We go down the hallway hitting each room as we get to it until we are at the doorway of the last room. As I start in, I see a body lying on the floor in front of me. I can see that the person is burned almost beyond recognition as I crawl past and put the last of the fire out. As the smoke clears and we can stand up, we take a better look. It appears to be a man and he is curled up in a fetal position. We are debating whether to move him or not when Forte comes in and says, "it looks like a lot of blood in the bathroom." We decide to wait for the police before we touch anything else.

The victim was 74 years old and he had been shot, had his throat cut and been set on fire. Two younger men had been sharing the apartment with him for the last few months and evidently there had been an argument and that was their way of ending it. The first two cops on the scene were two guys that hung in our station all the time and were well known to all of us. One officer looked at the victim and declared that it was the worst case of suicide he had ever seen. The cop's sense of humor was sicker than ours and that's saying something. By the time we cleared the fire ground and got back to the station the sun was coming up, another night where my head never hit the pillow. It will feel good to crawl into my own bed when I get home and sleep until it is time to get up and come back in. My gloves should be dry by then and Captain Zimmer can stop laughing at me.

A few weeks later, we are still on a roll when it comes to working fires. Last shift we had three fires in one day, two were working fires and one was a mattress fire. We are on day work now and it has been quiet all morning, not one run yet, when suddenly there is a loud banging on the firehouse door. A young boy says there is a fire down the street in the apartments on the corner of Madison and McMechen. These are garden style apartments, fairly new, made of brick. Nowhere near as combustible as most of the houses in the neighborhood. We turn out and go the short distance to the apartment and we can see the smoke blowing out the second floor window. I lead off as Doug is on the pipe today and he is already masking up in preparation for his attack on the fire. We have a very short lead and it does not take me long to mask up and join him in his crawl down the hallway. Mitch Johnson, who is acting today, is having trouble with his mask and I pass him in the hallway. I snuggle up behind Doug and we are making our way towards the bedroom that is fully involved. The flames are licking out the doorway ten feet and the smoke is down to the floor. Doug makes his way into the doorway beating back the flames as he goes when some moron from Engine 1, outside with a hose, opens his pipe into the room we are in.

This immediately pushes the heat and flames right back at us and Doug involuntarily lunges backwards into me. We both tumble out into the hallway and regroup to make another attempt. I'm talking to Doug, just letting him know I'm still behind him, and we start in again. He is about five feet into the room when the drop ceiling, which is burning, falls and a large burning ember goes right down his boot and is burning the hell out of his leg. He is really scrambling around now, trying to shoot some water down his boot, while at the same time not take the water off the ceiling. This turns out to be impossible and we wind up out in the hallway again. I grab the pipe and stick it down his boot and open it up and I can almost hear him sigh with relief. I now have the pipe and he is behind me so we decide to give it another try. The entire ceiling is now down so I don't have to worry about the same thing happening again.

I manage to knock the rest of the fire down but now my bell is going off letting me know that I'm almost out of air. I make my way to the nearest window, take off my helmet so I can take my mask off, and I stick my head out the window to get some air. At the same exact time, Forte and Fred Hill from Truck 4 are throwing the 24-foot aluminum ladder to that window. Because of the smoke, they can't see me and I can't see them and the end of the ladder hits me right between the eyes. It is enough to briefly knock me out and I fall back into the room. Somebody helps me up and out of the building, where I run into Doug waiting for the ambo. At first I don't want to go to the hospital but when I bend over to get a drink of water I almost fall flat on my face. I go to Mercy Hospital and after an examination they tell me I have a concussion. I could have told them that, after all, I just had one last week playing football; but I don't mention it because I never reported it. We didn't exactly fight that fire in a textbook manner but the bottom line is the fire went out. That didn't stop me from calling the moron that stuck the pipe in the window when I came back to work and cussing him out. What he did was break a cardinal rule; you never stick a pipe in the window when there is somebody inside.

CHAPTER 21
Another Job Well Done

The next big fire in Baltimore was on May 15th, C-shift was off duty, and we missed one of the most life threatening fires in Baltimore history. Shortly before 7 a.m. on a Sunday morning, a fire was reported in the Sherwood Hotel in the 200 block of Monument Street. The fire had started in the laundry room and when firefighters arrived, flames were roaring through the four story building, killing three people and injuring more than two dozen others. Nine alarms were pulled bringing more than 150 firefighters and 60 pieces of equipment to the scene. A lot of the guests were elderly and some were jumping from windows as high as the fourth floor when firefighters pulled up. One man jumped from the fourth floor and landed on the marquee in front of the hotel breaking his back, although he survived. Two people were found dead on the fourth floor and one on the first floor. When the first firefighters arrived, there were numerous people hanging out of windows getting ready to jump. They could not get to everybody at once and it was tough convincing some of them not to jump but to wait their turn to be rescued. Acting Chief Geoghagen said, "we eventually laddered the whole building and we got everybody out that it was physically possible to get out." Firefighter Palmer from Truck 1 crawled across a ladder that had been thrown from an adjoining building across an alley four floors up to the hotel. He found an unconscious man and dragged him back across the ladder where mouth to mouth was performed on the victim and he was resuscitated. The men from Truck 1 and Engine 32 were credited with rescuing 25 people. Thirteen firefighters were hurt during the fire, suffering from burns and smoke inhalation. There were 75 people living at the hotel at the time of the fire. Considering that the fire was on a Sunday morning when all the residents were sleeping, the loss of only three people was remarkable. It was one hell of a job by everybody on the fire ground and there were numerous awards given out in the aftermath of the fire.[7]

The next night we were working and I was driving Battalion Chief 4, Chief Downing. There were still a lot of companies on the hotel fire ground overhauling early in the evening when a box was struck out for a dwelling fire in the first block of North Fulton Avenue. We were six blocks away and you could see the smoke in the sky. We pulled up in front of a three story vacant dwelling that was fully involved with occupied dwellings on either side of it. It did not surprise me when shortly after we arrived, Chief Downing told me to ask for a second alarm. We had exposure problems on both sides and a tremendous amount of fire. As the second alarm companies were arriving, Chief

[7] Blatchley, R. (1977, May 15). 3 Die as Blaze Roars Through Midtown Hotel. *The Baltimore Sun.*

Downing told me to get one of the truck companies to ventilate the dwelling to the right of the fire building. I grabbed Truck 23 and told them what the chief had said.

I was standing in front of the dwelling that needed to be ventilated and I watched as they started for the front door. I turned my back to the dwelling and started to walk away when I heard a bang like a screen door slamming. I turned to see what it was when suddenly the entire front of the three-story house blew off. The force of the explosion knocked me to my knees and I skidded to a stop near Engine 36. I looked in disbelief at the dwelling. Every brick and every window was blown off the front of it and was in a big pile at the front of the building. I crawled up into the front seat of Engine 36, which was a second line engine with no roof on it, and I had to push the debris off the front seat to get to the radio. I asked for a third alarm but there were so many companies trying to go in service from the hotel fire to take our fire that I couldn't get through. I finally said "Battalion Chief 4 urgent," and the radio traffic stopped. I then asked for a third alarm. I didn't know where the Chief was but I knew we needed more help. It turned out that the Chief was around back when it blew and he started running around front to see what happened. Unfortunately, Smitty [you see any bugs up there] from Engine 38 was running in the opposite direction to get away from the blast. He and the Chief collided at the corner of the building. Since Smitty is 6'3 and the Chief is 5'9, the Chief got the worst of it. He did manage to come around front and tell me to ask for a third alarm. I didn't tell him I already had, I just said "okay" and went to help look for the members of Truck 23. We did not know if they were in the building when it blew or not.

We thought they might be under the debris out front and a bunch of us started digging frantically at the pile. After a few minutes, it was discovered that all the guys from Truck 23 were alright, just cuts and bruises and probably some stained shorts. The explosion was caused by a backup of heated gasses in a dwelling that had been recently renovated with new windows and it was almost airtight. We also were one truck short on the first alarm due to a mix-up at communications because of all the companies at the Sherwood Hotel. Before it was over, we had lost all three dwellings to the fire and Chief Downing had to go to the hospital for chest pains. I had to go to Engine 18 to pick up the Captain to finish out the night as acting battalion chief. The next night on a trash fire in a vacant dwelling, Forte kicked out the plywood that was used to board up the windows and the noise made me jump like I had been shot. I was gun shy for about a month after that.

Starting an interior attack on a dwelling fire. (Unknown)

Part II

Working on the East Side

CHAPTER 22
Contract Negotiations

The union and the city are at odds over our latest contract, so what else is new? But this time I think the mayor has gone too far. We are in the second year of a two-year contract, that had been signed a year earlier, and the mayor has decided not to honor the second year. This means no raises again. When I and everybody that followed me into the fire department were hired, we were guaranteed a $500 raise each year for four years and a $1,000 raise in the fifth year. This would bring everybody up to top paid firefighter after five years. This was on all the flyers advertising the job of firefighter and it was something all firefighters looked forward to. The mayor has also decided not to pay us what we have coming to us. This means that some guys may never reach top pay. It does not affect me, I went to top pay last year, but the hundreds of guys that were hired after me in the last four years are very upset. We know we are right but right has nothing to do with what the city does to us every year. I don't understand how Mayor Schaefer can do this to the most loyal, dedicated, hardest working employees he has. Why don't they understand that we are putting our lives on the line every time we go out the door? I would like to take the mayor into a burning building with me one time and let him see what we do every day, and then let him tell me we don't deserve to get a decent raise or at least our increments to top pay. Hyman Pressman, the city comptroller, said "I think it's unfair to make the employees bear the brunt of all the troubles city government has gotten into-it's a financial rut. We have a contract with them and they are not going to get what we promised them." "I hope there is no strike," Mr. Pressman continued. "I appeal to the firefighters not to strike." He sympathized with their complaints, however, saying, "You have been abused, you have gotten a raw deal." I have never seen my fellow firefighters so angry. It would not surprise me if there was a strike. We have the first of two union meetings tonight and I'm going to go and listen to what Larry Nelson, our president, has to say. In Annapolis, the acting governor has alerted the National Guard about the possibility of a strike.[13]

The union meeting was wild, guys were screaming about getting screwed out of their money and the vote was taken quickly. There were only about 300 of us there, the majority will vote at the next meeting, but our vote was to strike. We are fed up with being treated like a ghetto dog at contract time. We've been kicked enough and decided that it's time to bite back. I don't think the final outcome will be good for us. I remember what the city did to the cops

---

[13] Riddle, C. (1977, July 1) Firemen Vote for Job Action. Firemen Return to Work in Face of Layoff Threat. *The Baltimore Sun, pp 1A*

that went on strike a few years back, they were all fired, but the final vote will be tomorrow night.

I went to the second meeting even though I had already voted, just to hear what the majority had to say. There were over 900 firefighters there and the meeting was just as raucous as the first but cooler heads prevailed at the end. We voted to have a job action instead of a strike. Each day and each night when we report for work, we will all go to the fire department infirmary and complain about a cold or whatever and have to be examined. While we are doing this, the shift that's working will be getting overtime, and then when they come back to work they will do the same thing as we did. There will be no reports written and no maintenance on the vehicles. That way the city will never be placed in danger and maybe we can get our point across. There will not be a staffing shortage on the engines and trucks.

We did our job action for six days and then the city found a judge that ruled we were endangering the city even though we weren't. They threatened the union with a $10,000 a day fine and jail for the union leaders if we kept it up, so we capitulated. Hundreds of guys got screwed out of their money and the bitterness will last a long time. I doubt that the relationship we had with the city, although it was never that good to begin with, will ever be repaired. The city made it clear that "no matter what we promise you, we are not obligated to honor that contract." When all this was going on, the mayor parked his limo in front of the firehouse at Eutaw and Lombard and went across the street for a sandwich. When he returned there was a bumper sticker on his limo that said Baltimore's worst mayor, William Donald Schaefer. He saw it and was enraged; he went into the firehouse and demanded to know who did it. No one would tell him but a lot of people knew who it was. In the end, the fire department kicked Mitch Powers from Truck 2 out of the firehouse and sent him to Truck 8 as punishment. He never admitted to it and they could not prove it but they knew it was him. A small victory for us. Another firefighter at Truck 13 refused to shake the mayor's hand and told him that, "after what you have done to my family, I cannot shake your hand." He was promptly shipped to Engine 50. The Chief was told to ship them out as punishment. The order came down from higher up but no one knew how high up. We feel betrayed by the mayor and there is a lot of anger in the department. Morale is lower than I've ever seen it.

The following was written by Michael Olesker on July 8, 1977 for the News American. It is titled *Putting Out The Fires But Not The Heat.*[14]

> Four times in the dark hours the panic calls came. Once, a match dropped into a stuffed chair ignited a living room. Twice, pots of food boiled over and set off blazes. Once, the alarm was false. Four races against the steaming night. "A quiet night," Sam Woods said. "Real quiet," Bill Turnage agreed. There were six of them sitting here now at Truck Company 13

14 Olesker, M. (1977, July 8). Putting Out the Fires but Not the Heat. *The News American*

on S. Carey Street. It was early morning after this quiet night, and most of these men were just coming off a routine 14 hour shift in the heat. But the heat was still on at Truck Co. 13 and at firehouses across the city of Baltimore. The heat is aimed at the Mayor who last week took firemen for granted and ignored a contract already negotiated. "The mayor can hang it up with us now," Charles Cannon was saying now. "We're never going to trust that guy again." "It's always the same story," said Sam Woods. "The mayor says, work with me, and I'll help you next time. And next time, we get screwed again." And around the table inside Truck Co. 13 now, the talk was dark and full of anger. It's the same old story; the people who matter in this city – the cops, the firemen, the teachers, the ones who make real contributions to people's lives – they're the ones who always are treated like orphans at contract time. And there is almost no recourse. The mayor pleads poverty, except in election years. The cops and the firemen are last lines of defense, so they are not supposed to walk out.

"We walk," said Calvin Washington, "and people 15 or 20 seconds from here die. And we are the only ones who can save them. They can try bringing in the National Guard but they aren't gonna save people like we do."

"And right there was the mayor's trump card," Charles Cannon said. "He knew we wouldn't walk. He knew we were going to be here."

He knew it so well that he could turn his back on a contract the firemen thought had been finalized. He knew it, and left them with no increases in their pay, and nothing they could do about it.

And almost none of the firemen you talk to believe what city officials declare – that if they'd gotten the money they wanted, other city employees would have to have been laid off.

"There's a great feeling of disbelief in all that talk," said Joe McDonald. "In fact, there's a great feeling of disbelief in the mayor."

"They are always telling us how special we are," said Sam Woods. He grunted over that.

The mayor knows how special Truck Co. 13 is. He came down to S. Carey St. last winter, in that brutal January, after the men from this company rescued 6 kids from a burning house in the 1800 block W. Baltimore Street.

> The mayor came down to S. Carey St. and gave out citations for heroism.
>
> "Yea," Frank Sagan said, "but you could see it that day when he was handing out those awards, he was saying, but don't get no ideas about money."
>
> "If he'd of told us back in January about the money," Calvin Washington said, "I believe we'd have walked than."
>
> Every month is rough on S. Carey St., but January was hell.
>
> This company was the second busiest in the city last year. They made 2,396 runs, many where lives hung in the balance.
>
> In January, there were 260 runs. The Company Truck is 20 years old and it is an open truck. In January, Joe McDonald said, "It was like riding a motorcycle in your pajamas."
>
> The cold came at them like an ax murderer. Men climbed onto roofs and found themselves skidding downward, out of control on winter ice.
>
> "It's rough," Frank Sagan said, "But it's rough all year. July 4th, we had 17 runs. You never stop. And you don't get a chance to be scared until it's too late."
>
> "That's right," Calvin Washington said, "You'll get back in bed and say, Jesus, what did I do out there?"
>
> There was sense of hurt in the room. They are unappreciated. They risk their lives, and the city turns their back on them.
>
> It's the old story. And not a pretty one either.

I could not have said it better myself. During the job action, there were numerous fires including a three alarm fire that destroyed the vacant third and fourth floors of the Franklin Hotel in the 400 block of Franklin Street. There was also a five alarm fire in the 1600 block of Thomas Avenue in West Baltimore. We took both on the second alarm on back-to-back days, July 3rd and 4th. And of course there was never a problem with response time or staffing, but despite this fact the judge still ruled that we were endangering the city. The fix was in and we all know it but the bottom line is, we lost as usual. Like I said earlier, a union that can't strike is not really a union, it's a social club. So despite the rhetoric and the posturing and also the hard work put in by the officers of the union, the outcome is almost always the same. The old adage, "you can't fight city hall" is still true but we will never stop trying. It makes us feel better to fight than to just roll over and play dead. The feeling in the firehouses is if Mayor Schaefer was on fire, we would not piss on him. The hard feelings will last a long, long time.

Despite the outcome of our contract dispute, we are still fighting the fires as aggressively as ever. We still make the interior attack that invariably leads to more injuries but less fire loss to the home owner. We do this because it is what we like to do not because of any loyalty to the city managers. The competitiveness between companies is still there, at least around where I work, and this seems a little crazy to me, but I am just as guilty as the next guy. The other day, Engine 13 and Engine 8 got to the front door of a vacant dwelling fire at the same time and started up the stairs with a line to the third floor at the same time. Captain Zimmer simply wrapped Engine 8's line around the stairway railing and that brought their pipe man to a screeching halt. Needless to say, I was able to reach the third floor first and get the fire. We all had a good laugh about that when we got back to quarters. Laughter is still the best medicine.

On December 2nd, we are on the street doing housing inspections looking for violations of fire codes. These violations are usually ignored by the residents and seem to be a colossal waste of time and energy. While doing our inspections, a fire is reported at the old Poly High School. Heavy fire is reported by the first-in company and we start to make our way in that direction. We are sure we will take it on the second alarm, we seem to take the whole city on the second alarm, and sure enough the Chief asks for it and away we go. When we get there, the flames are shooting out of two large front windows facing North Ave, reaching almost to the roof. However, the fire is in a fire resistant auditorium used for storage and it is knocked down pretty quickly. As we overhaul, Captain Zimmer tells Dougie Falls to pick up a 16-foot long ceiling hook and pull some of the ceiling. Dougie, who is 150 pounds soaking wet, looks at the Captain, smiles, and says "I'll tell you what Cap, you butt it and I'll raise it." I laughed so hard I almost choked on my chewing gum. How can you not love a guy like that?

CHAPTER 23
Burns

It was about this time that I burned my hand fighting a fire on Fremont Avenue near Presstman Street. We could see the smoke in the sky long before we reached the scene and we knew it was off good. We led off and reached the front door at about the same time as Engine 8 again. It looked as if the entire second floor was burning as we made our way onto the first floor and through the living room to the steps. Engine 8's pipe man and I stopped at the bottom of the stairs to mask up. In order to put my mask on I had to remove my gloves and when I had my mask on I looked at him and he was ready to go. The only problem was I didn't have my gloves back on yet so I said the hell with it and went ahead of him and up the stairs.

About halfway up I opened the pipe because the fire was blowing out the back room and into the hallway at the top of the stairs. I made my way to the top of the stairs and was turning toward the back room when someone hollered, "look out, it's behind you." I turned towards the steps in time to see the fire explode out of the ceiling of the stairwell I had just come up. I aimed my hose in that direction and gave it a good blast of water but it didn't seem to have much of an effect. Suddenly, the ceiling over my head erupted in flames and there was nowhere to go. I curled up in a ball and put the pipe straight up over my head. Burning pieces of ceiling were falling on me as I lay there curled up and I could hear someone asking me if I was okay. I knew my right hand was burning from the falling ceiling so I stuck it in front of the hose for a second to cool it off. I was knocking the fire down over my head slowly but surely and I eventually made my way into the back room and knocked that down too.

When I got the chance I asked Forte to shine his light on my hand but when he did, I was sorry I asked him. The skin had burned off my hand and was hanging from my fingertips like a spider web. My hand was bleeding but it really didn't hurt that bad. I knew I had to have it looked at. I made my way outside and walked to the ambo where they took one look at it and said I had to go to Mercy Hospital. They bandaged it up and we were just pulling away when somebody banged on the door and yelled to hold up a minute. We stopped and opened the back door to see Forte standing there. "Are you ok?" he said. "Yeah I'll survive," I said. "Good" he said, and then he smiled and said, "Can I have your lunch?" The old saying came back to me, never look for sympathy in a firehouse or a bar, as I laughed and told him to go ahead and eat it.

My hand had second and some third degree burns that took a long time to heal. One reason they took so long was because they got infected and the doctor had to rip the scab off and start over again. About a week after I was burned I had to make a return trip to the fire department infirmary to let them change the bandages. The doctor changed the bandages and then told me he was going to put me on regular duty but not to get my hand wet or dirty. I looked at him like he had two heads. "Do you know what I do for a living?" I asked him. "How the hell am I supposed to keep my hand dry and clean fighting fires?" I laughed as I walked away shaking my head, "I'm staying off until I heal," I said and I walked out. Compared to what some guys go through at the infirmary, this was just a minor glitch. There are some real horror stories in the department about the infirmary. I was off duty for a month while it healed and I was glad to get back to work.

CHAPTER 24
20 Seconds of Fame

The loss in contract negotiations was still the main topic of conversation in the firehouse even several months later, and one of the things that bothered everybody was that the public never got our side of the story. I thought about this and decided to go on a local television show called Speak Out on Channel 13. I wrote them a letter telling them what I wanted to say and to my surprise they answered my letter with one of their own. They said they would be glad to have me come in and tape what I had to say but that they would have to edit it first to make it fit the 20 second time allotted to me.

A week later, Lois and I went to the studio and were directed to a room to wait for someone to come and get us. "Are you nervous?" she asked me as we sat down. "No, not really, I'm still mad about what the city did to us and I'm looking forward to telling somebody how I feel, even if it's just for 20 seconds." Ten minutes later we were escorted into the room where they do the local news broadcast and I sat down at the news desk. Lois was taken to the control booth and would watch from there. I took a deep breath and started.

"Why is it that when Baltimore City firefighters slowed down on house work and went en mass to the infirmary it was considered a strike and dangerous? We were still fighting fires and saving lives. The only danger was to ourselves as we entered burning buildings. The purpose of the slowdown was to try to get raises the mayor had promised us. He stated that there's no money in the city for his employees. Yet money is found in the budget for a park that is 11 miles outside the city limits and to build a sailboat [the Pride of Baltimore]. Whatever happened to the priorities in this city? Our taxes go up because of the mayor's frivolous spending on his pet projects while the services that people need, such as police and fire protection and sanitation services decline because of a lack of funds. One of the mayor's favorite slogans is *Your City Cares*. Who's he trying to kid!"

I had to have my name on the screen and they wanted to put firefighter in front of it but I told them no, I was there as a private tax paying citizen. This turned out to be a wise decision. The tape would be aired once a day but more if there was a reaction to it from the public. It turned out that it was aired three times a day for seven days. After that week, I was pulled aside by an officer in the fire department who was a friend of mine. He told me to be careful and not to screw up because the powers downtown were waiting for me and they were going to stick it to me if they had the chance. I guess I got my point across. They say you can judge a person by his enemies so I must be doing something right!

Early in the new year, Captain Zimmer is promoted to Chief and we wish him luck. We will miss him; he was a lot of fun to work with and a very good firefighter. His replacement is Captain Sturm but he will not be on our shift, due to acting purposes he will be on B-shift and we will get a young Lieutenant named Chris McKinnon. McKinnon is the youngest Lieutenant in the history of the fire department. He is gung-ho which is good for us and he is cocky which might or might not be good for us. Time will tell but we have serious reservations about Captain Sturm. I think we will be glad he is not on our shift. He comes to us with the reputation of being someone who likes to stir up controversy. The rest of our shift is intact; myself, Stan Williams, Chris Foster, Mitch Johnson, Ron Jenkins and Jack Sterret on the engine. The truck is Lt. Crawford, a regular in the card games, Pete Thomas and Fred Hill are the driver and Tillerman, Brian Jones, Charles Forte and Bob Smalls make up the rest of the crew.

On February 15th, C-shift was off and B-shift was working day work when at 2 p.m. a box came in for a fire reported at the Beethoven Apartments at the corner of Park Ave. and McMechen Street. The Beethoven was a renovated apartment building, five stories high in what could be called a yuppie neighborhood. It consisted of two separate buildings, the North and South, which were divided by a heavy duty fire wall. The fire was in the North building and had been started by a 10 year old boy searching for a toy under his bed with a candle. When the bed caught fire, he ran out of the building and across the street to a drug store to call his mother. This gave the fire a real good head start. Engine 13 was on another run when the box was struck out and did not take it until the second alarm was struck out, but there was plenty of fire left. By the time it was over, there were nine alarms in and one dead police officer. When the first units arrived, they found heavy smoke conditions on the second floor and fire blowing out the windows of one of the apartments. The fire was thought to be contained by the first alarm until it was found running through false wall partitions and which allowed it to get into the space next to the elevator shafts. By 2:30 p.m., it had burst through the roof and the floors were starting to buckle. Three members of Engine 25 were briefly trapped and slightly burned when a ceiling fell on them. About this time, it was decided to pull everybody out and surround and drown.

More than 175 firefighters and about 50 pieces of equipment were used to fight the fire and it took four and a half hours to bring it under control. We came in on night work at 4 p.m. and relieved a tired B-shift. It was still raging through the roof at this time and we had a lot of work left to do. When the fire was first reported, Officer Paulie Brooks was patrolling nearby. He ran into the building and twice carried kids to safety but the third time he went in, he got trapped. The last that was heard from him was when he called on his walkie-talkie and said, "help, I'm trapped on the third floor." His radio then went dead at the start of a garbled transmission that his fellow officers thought the words "rear elevator" were mentioned. Officer Brooks was well known to all of us at Engine 13 because he often did his paperwork and ate his lunch with us. Eventually the roof and fifth through the first floor collapsed into the basement in the center of the building, right where the elevator was. The search for Officer Brooks's body continued well into the night until he was finally located in the basement in what was left of the rear elevator. The cables had snapped from the heat of the fire and the elevator had plummeted to the basement with him in it. I was there when they brought his remains out but it was mostly just his gun belt, his badge and pieces of his uniform. He was 33 years old with one child and a step-child. He died a hero trying to rescue people but he had made a fatal mistake when he got on the elevator. That's the last place you want to go in a fire. There were 77 people made homeless by the blaze. We were relieved on the fire ground the next morning by B-shift again. It was a long night for us and also for the officers that kept a vigil for their fellow officer until he was found around 5 in the morning.

We are back down to the high rises again today; this time it is at 851 George Street for the trash chute. We are walking across the sidewalk on the George St. side of the building when suddenly half of a watermelon comes crashing down from the upper floors and just misses Chris Foster. I swear it would have killed him if it had hit him. We should have been more alert. Just last week, Jim Imor from Engine 38 was hit by a bottle thrown from the upper floor of one of the high rises on Lexington Street. It bounced off the side of his helmet and cut his face sending him into a rage. He grabbed the cop that was nearest him and tried to get his gun out of his holster. When asked later what he was trying to do, he replied, "I was just gonna start shooting until I hit somebody." We really have not had much trouble at the high rises lately but I still make sure I have my helmet on no matter what the call is for. Better to be safe than sorry.

CHAPTER 25
The Beat Goes On

On May 24th, B-shift was working day work when they had another serious fire with loss of life involved. This one was right up the street from Engine 8 and Truck 10 in the 1000 block of Gilmor Street.[15] The fire was just one alarm and was under control in 30 minutes but it claimed the life of two children and their mother. It started on the first floor in the dining room and quickly spread up the stairs and consumed both bedrooms. Before the first firefighters arrived on the scene, the mother had thrown a baby out the second floor window to the pavement below. The little boy, who was only 9 months old, received head and chest injuries and was in critical condition. The mother and two other children were found just ten minutes after the fire had started, huddled near a second floor window. The mother had the three year old in her arms. All three were pronounced dead at the hospital. I don't think the average person realizes how fast a fire moves once it has a good start. You never have as much time as you think you do to get out and the visibility goes from good to zero in a matter of seconds.

And the beat goes on. On August 26th, we go on the fourth alarm to the 600 block of Lexington Street for what turns out to be a six-alarm fire in the old Koester's bakery. It is a stubborn fire that takes over two hours to bring under control in suffocating heat. On October 24th, another six-alarm fire, this one fought by A-shift. This fire could have been devastating for the fire department. It was in the vacant double loft building at 102-104 Hopkins Place. Evidently, it had been burning for quite some time before the fire department was called. The call was received at communications at 5:17 p.m. for smoke seeping out the roof-line on the five story building. A group of firefighters had already entered the building and was on the way up when "the roof exploded in flames," according to one eyewitness. This fire was similar to the one we had in February 1976 at 106-108 Hopkins Place that went to nine alarms. Eight firefighters were hurt when the roof exploded in flames. Dennis Dougherty was treated for first and second degree burns to the hands and legs. Richard Armstrong was treated for burns to the face and hands. Another firefighter burned his elbow and firefighters Earl Miller, Richard Lindsay, Robert Cavero and David Ernest were all treated for back injuries. Firefighters were able to save the B&O office building next door by going to the roof of it and pouring water across the narrow alley onto the original fire building. The B&O building was eight stories high; if that had caught fire who knows where the fire would have stopped. I think the department dodged a bullet on this one; we could have very easily lost some guys on this fire. The bravery and

15 (1978, May 25) – Mother, 2 Children Killed in House Fire; 2 Others Injured. *The Baltimore Sun, pp 1D*

commitment to the job at hand of the men in this department is amazing. Too bad the mayor chooses to ignore it.

Ray Lockett and Donald Horton helping Engine 8 with a 2 1/2 inch hose. (Jim Keefe)

CHAPTER 26
Another Great Job

Another six-alarm fire hit on October 29th and this fire could have very easily killed dozens of people but for the efforts of the firefighters. It was Sunday and the day you turn the clocks back an hour and we had been busy most of the night. At 6 a.m., we were all in bed when the gong went off for the tenth time that night. We turned out quickly as we heard the man on watch hollering, "Carver Hall Apartments, Lafayette and Division Streets." We had been there many times for pots of food, mattresses and an occasional apartment fire, but we were not prepared for what we saw when we turned the corner this time. The Carver Apartments was a four story building half a block long that had been cut up into as many apartments as was possible to squeeze in there. There were no sprinklers and the alarm bells only went off when they felt like it and were ignored by everybody that lived there. The building faced Division Street, and Lafayette Avenue ran along the South side of it. The building had a lot of deep alcoves on the sides and in the front of it, with a narrow ledge that ran around the fourth floor under the windows. We were first in and when we pulled up, there were a number of people perched on this ledge preparing to jump to the courtyard below. Heavy smoke was pouring from every window we could see and there was a woman climbing down from the third floor on sheets she had tied together. All this was going on, on the south side of the building. In the front it was much of the same, people were hanging out of windows screaming for help as the flames were blowing out windows next to them. There were some people trapped on the roof and flames were shooting through the roof, leaving them with nowhere to go. Six alarms were sounded within 16 minutes as we started our rescue efforts.

We made no attempt to take a line in; everybody on the first alarm was committed to rescue operations. Truck 4 was on Lafayette Avenue and was going to try to pluck the people off the fourth floor ledge. However, when they raised their aerial ladder and extended it into the alcove, it would not sustain its own weight and slowly dropped below the ledge. As I remember it, Truck 4 was old and had failed the ladder test at fire school twice but because of budget restrictions no new truck was ordered. Now this decision by the powers that be could get a number of people killed. Three times the aerial ladder was raised and three times it dropped before it reached the people. Finally, this attempt was aborted and the aerial ladder was raised to an adjacent two-story building. From there, a 24-foot ladder was carried up and thrown to the ledge of the fire building. The people on the ledge then had to slide across the ledge to where the ladder was and come down that way.

I ran around front and was grabbed by Paul Alisea, a firefighter from Truck 10, who asked me to help with the throwing of the 50-foot extension ladder to the roof. The only way to get close enough to where the people were trapped on the roof was to throw the ladder in one of the alcoves. This precluded the use of the tormentor poles attached to the sides of the ladder and which are supposed to be used when you raise it. Six of us muscled it up and Paul Alisea started pulling on the halyard to extend it to the roof. He got it extended to the roof but the people on the roof couldn't wait for it to be lowered onto the edge of the roof and started to climb on the wrong side of it. We hollered to them to back off and we leaned it onto the edge of the roof. Paul and I started up the ladder and had gotten almost to the roof when Truck 11, coming on the second alarm, came screaming around the corner. They saw what we were doing and stopped the truck to see if they could help. The driver threw the aerial ladder to the roof and we decided that it would be a lot easier to take everybody down the aerial than on our steep 50' ground ladder.

While all this was going on, firefighters were using ground ladders to rescue people from windows on the third and fourth floors and the third alarm companies were starting to get some hoses in the front door. The first two alarms had been doing nothing but rescues. When it was finally over, it was estimated that we had rescued over 50 people without the loss of one single life. It was a great job by everyone involved. After we were relieved and got back to the station the stories started flowing since we had all done something different to help with the rescues. I don't think there has ever been a fire in Baltimore where more people were rescued with not one single fatality.

CHAPTER 27
Question "O"

Negotiations with the city have become impossible again so we have decided to put it to a citywide vote. We are going to try to get binding arbitration through a ballot referendum. It will be called question "O" on the ballot and the voters will decide if we should get it or not. What it does is bring in a neutral arbitrator to solve the impasse and he must take one side or the other and his decision is final. It should make the city at least put a decent offer on the table. If they don't and we do, the decision should go in our favor. The city is fighting this tooth and nail because they know they have been sticking it up our ass for years and they don't want that to change. We will be working the polls all over Baltimore to convince the public that it is a good idea. If we don't get it, I would not be surprised to see a strike in the near future. The following is another Michael Olesker column in the News American paper dated Nov. 4, 1977. It is titled "Fire Alarm Unanswered."

> The firefighters keep getting burned. No job is more murderous. The firefighter crawls on his belly into buildings, and the heat sinks so deeply in his pores that his skin seems to melt. If he has time to fasten his mask, he's got a break. If he doesn't, smoke enters the lungs and works its way through the bloodstream to the brain. Forget modern technology. You still have to fight a fire the old way: get as close as possible and put water on it.
>
> But the firefighters keep getting burned when they shouldn't. They get burned when they sit down with the city of Baltimore to fasten a contract. The last time they did this everybody shook hands and agreed it wasn't a fabulous contract, but at least the raises were something.
>
> But they were nothing.
>
> When it comes to spending money on the people that matter - the firemen, the police, the schoolteachers - the city finds it very convenient to plead poverty.
>
> Fifteen months ago, Mayor Schaefer said the city could not afford to pay increments to the firefighters. Forget the contract, forget the handshakes. The city simply was not going to pay.
>
> For this kind of good faith, you have maybe three-quarters of the firefighters of Baltimore City working moonlight jobs to make ends meet. "July 1, 1977, the mayor took away our incre-

> ments," said Bob Dodderlein, of Engine 44. I was due my last increment July 13, and they just decided to stop paying." So after 6½ years belching smoke, Dodderlein still makes $13,300 a year. "Part time I'm a laborer for a brick layer", he said. "I leave the firehouse and I've got just enough time to make it to the brick laying job. I'm not home for four days and four nights at a time. I have to abandon my family to support my family; it's as simple as that."
>
> The themes, again and again, were these; you can't have people doing the meanest work in creation for no money; and you can't bargain in good faith with the city. The firefighters want binding arbitration in their contracts. That's question O on Tuesday's ballot.[16]

He went on to talk about our problems with the city over the years and he pushed for question O on the ballot.

On November 8th, the people went to the polls and voted overwhelmingly for Question O. If nothing else comes from this, at least we beat the city on something. It feels good and I'm sure that Olesker's column helped a lot. Now only time will tell.

On December 18th, we are just finishing our housework when a box is struck out for a dwelling fire in the 700 block of Newington Avenue in Reservoir Hill. Reservoir Hill is made up of mostly very large three story row houses that at one time were homes to some of the more influential people in the city. Now "the hill" is blighted and run down and the large row homes have been cut up into numerous one and two room apartments. When we go up there, we never know what to expect. Sometimes we go in the front door and find that it won't lead us to the second floor. We have to go around back to get to the second floor front. It is like being in a maze at times, and under smoky conditions it can be a nightmare.

As we are going up Eutaw Street with sirens wailing and the air horn blasting, we are all looking at the skies for a telltale sign of smoke. There is none visible but the police helicopter is circling in the air above the hill and I make a bet with Stan that we have a fire. As we cross North Avenue, we can see smoke in the sky but it does not look too bad. As we turn onto Newington Avenue, it is a different story. We are confronted with heavy black smoke pouring out of the third floor and there are three people lying on the sidewalk in front of the house.

As we stop to lead off, Truck 4 goes around us to take the rear, Truck 11 is in the front and the aerial ladder is already out of the bed and going up. The first engine on the scene is Engine 1 and they are heading for the front door with their line. After we drop our lead-off line and start down the street, I can see that one of the people on the sidewalk is actually a baby around 4 years

[16] Olesker, M (1978, November 4) Fire Alarm Unanswered. *The News American*

old and she is not moving. I glance up at the aerial ladder just in time to see Ben Forrest, the driver of Truck 11, go in the window on the third floor. He emerges seconds later carrying an unconscious infant in his arms and makes his way down the aerial ladder. We take a line in to back up Engine 1 and make our way up to the third floor. Engine 1 has crawled into the front room and knocked down the bulk of the fire and we go to the left and hit the fire that has spread to the rear room.

By the time we finish up and make our way outside, all the victims have been removed and are on their way to the hospital. The little girl had been thrown from the third floor by her mother in an attempt to save her. She had been taken to Provident Hospital with burns, a skull fracture, and a broken leg. Another person was in critical condition after jumping from the third floor. She had skull and facial fractures. The other person outside was the child's mother but no one knew how she had gotten out of the house. She had burns and cuts, but was otherwise unhurt.

Prior to the arrival of the fire department, police officers were told that a child was still on the third floor and they made an attempt to reach the third floor but were driven back by the smoke. This was the child that Ben had rescued just in time to save her life. She was suffering from smoke inhalation but was expected to live. The fire had started in the apartment when grease had spilled onto the stove and spread to the walls. The mother echoed what a lot of people say when they escape from a fire, "I can't believe how fast it spread." Unless you experience it, you are always shocked to see how quickly fire can spread. As we slowly made our way back to our station, I couldn't help but think how lucky that little girl was that Ben had the presence of mind to put the aerial ladder to the window instead of to the roof. It is a great feeling for Ben to know that he was directly responsible in the saving of a life. I think how lucky I am to be in a job that allows us to experience that feeling. There is nothing like it.

CHAPTER 28
Snowed In

On my birthday, December 13th, my shift is off but an unknown arsonist is hard at work in downtown Baltimore. In less than six hours, two fires are set at the Lord Baltimore Hotel at the corner of Baltimore Street and Fayette Street. The second fire goes to five alarms and forces the evacuation of everyone at the hotel. Smoke was pouring out of the sixth floor windows when the first companies arrived on the scene. The smoke made its way throughout the building all the way to the 22nd floor. Most of the cast from "Hello Dolly" were staying there and had to be evacuated, including Carol Channing. It was another excellent job by the members of the fire department.

On February 18, 1979, it started to snow and it turned into a full-scale blizzard before it was done. I was off but the department would face some very tough days and nights ahead. As the snow mounted, the police department's ability to respond was diminished because of a lack of 4-wheel drive vehicles. When the good citizens of Baltimore realized that the cops couldn't move, they decided to start looting and burning places of business. A dwelling fire on Gold Street that had nothing to do with the looting, caused one firefighter to be taken to the hospital. He was being transported by a Battalion Chief because the ambos were all either busy or stuck in the snow. As the Chief passed the Mace Lumber Yard on Fremont Ave in West Baltimore, he saw people carrying paint cans from the looted store. A few minutes later the store was blazing away and units were fighting their way through the snow-covered streets to get there. Some companies were not able to get closer than three blocks away before they got bogged down in the deep snow. The men grabbed all the tools they could carry and ran to the fire. Some companies never even made it to the fire at all and other companies had to be dispatched in their place.

The Lumber Yard fire would go to four alarms and Chief Curtis said it would have been worse but for the efforts of the first engine on the scene. Engine 8 was working with six men instead of four because the men could not get home and stayed at the firehouse. This company put their monitor pipe, or deck gun as it's called, to use right away and this was credited with helping to control the spread of the fire.

In East Baltimore, it was more of the same. The Lewis Furniture Company sat on the corner of Patterson Park Avenue and Gay Street. It had been looted three times over the course of the night and there was nothing left to steal so it was set on fire. Deep snow and abandoned cars made it almost impossible to reach the scene. "We had to go eight blocks out of our way to get here," said Captain Blick from Truck 5. When the companies made it to the scene, they were met with high snow banks to climb over and treacherous footing to try to place their ladders on. The flames reached as high as 75 feet in the air at the height of the fire. The collapse of part of the roof caused firefighters to flee a second floor storage area where they were battling the flames.[17] The fire started at 9:30 at night and raged out of control for most of the night. The two-story building with two big wings of storage space was totally destroyed. What was once a viable place of business in a tough neighborhood is now gone. I expect the people will complain in the near future about no place to shop. This is like the boy who killed his parents and then asked for mercy because he was an orphan. It is no wonder businesses are fleeing the city in record numbers.

All the while the looting was going on, Mayor Schaefer was on television telling everybody the city was calm. A-shift at Truck 4 and Engine 13 were on night work watching the 11 o'clock news. As they watched the looting one of the men smirked as he said, "Yeah, the Mayor's got everything under control." The contract bitterness remains the main topic of conversation around the firehouse and the mayor's problems during the snow riots do not go unnoticed without some satisfaction by everybody present.

17 Brown, D. (1979, February 21) Slick Streets, cars Slow Firefighting Efforts. *The Baltimore Sun, pp A5*

CHAPTER 29
Black and White

In January 1979, we have an arsonist working in our district now and he is raising hell. Day and night he strikes vacant buildings with no regard for the people that live on either side. We fight vacant dwellings much the same as occupied, interior attack, unless the building is completely unsafe to enter. The arsonist seems to be trying to hurt firefighters because he is cutting holes in floors just inside windows or doors. We are now being a little more careful as we enter theses firetraps.

The other day, Ron Green, from Engine 13, was driving the Chief when they spotted a fire on Division Street. The box had not even been struck out yet when they pulled around the corner in time to see a guy in the doorway of the vacant dwelling on fire. He turned around and ran back inside as Ron and the chief stopped in front. "Go get him," the Chief said and Ron jumped out of the car in hot pursuit. He ran in the house and up the stairs after the arsonist but stopped when he got to the second floor landing. The guy he was chasing was standing there staring at the fire he had started on the second floor. The look on his face was as vacant as the dwelling he had set on fire. Ron came back downstairs and told the Chief "that guy's crazy, you want him, you go get him." The chief had already asked for the box and was not inclined to go in the house after the guy. They knew he would have to come out sooner or later. It turned out he escaped out the back door as the engines pulled up out front. I don't think he was ever caught but his fires stopped after that incident and that was a welcome relief. There are some really strange people on this earth and a lot of them reside in our first alarm district.

I have worked with a lot of black firefighters since I've been in the department. There was James Schuster, Jim Sanders, and Jacob Clark on my shift at Engine 25, not to mention all the black guys in other companies I worked with at various times. At Engine 13 and Truck 4, I worked with Bob Smalls, Fred Hill, and Jack Sterret. I was shocked one day when a friend of mine, not in the fire department, asked me how the black firefighters were on the fire ground. He wanted to know if they carried their weight when it came to doing all the dangerous work we did. I couldn't believe he had asked me that. It had never occurred to me that someone would think that. Some of the best firefighters I have ever worked with were black. Bob Smalls was fearless and I knew if I was in trouble, he would be one of the first ones to come and get me.

When you are crawling down a smoke-filled hallway, you are not thinking about the color of the guy's skin that is on the roof opening up. In my mind you either do the job or you don't do the job. You are a good firefighter or you are a bum, and the decision to be one or the other is yours. And make no mistake about it, there are some bums in the fire department, just like any other job, but skin color has nothing to do with it. There have been guys I worked with that I didn't think much of on a personal level but they were damn good firefighters and that was the bottom line. Fred Hill and I have running arguments all the time about a variety of subjects such as the death penalty, I'm in favor of it, he is not, and our tastes in music are far apart, but if he were in trouble on a fire, I would put my life on the line to get him out and he would do the same for me.

Jack Sterret is one of the finest people I've ever had the pleasure to work with. We compete against each other in basketball and on the card table like it is the championship of the free world and I'm proud to call him a friend. When I'm on the fire ground my only concern is, can I trust a guy to do what has to be done. When you put people together of different races, with different views on a variety of subjects, you are bound to have some arguments and disagreements. But when it comes to doing the job, I have never seen a difference in the work because this guy is black or that guy is white. It was a ridiculous question that didn't even deserve an answer but I answered it anyway.

CHAPTER 30
Rocks, Bottles, and False Alarms

On March 5th, there was a terrible accident involving Engine 54 and Truck 30. The accident was only four blocks from my home at the intersection of Plainfield Avenue and Antenna Avenue, a blind intersection with four way stop signs. Both companies left the house at the same time responding to a street box that had been pulled false. According to the fire department Safety Officer, Truck 30 was east bound on Antenna and Engine 54 was south bound on Plainfield when they came together with a tremendous crash. There was a large hedge surrounding the house on the corner that prevented them from seeing each other as they approached from opposite directions. The pump operator, Matthew Carson, was thrown through the windshield and landed under Truck 30 but survived with numerous injuries. The acting Lieutenant on Engine 54, Pat Reed, was trapped in the wreckage for twenty minutes before he could be pulled out. He was in a coma until he passed away two weeks later. What a tragic waste of a life.

The box the companies were responding to was on the corner of LaSalle and Mayfield Avenues and had been pulled false many times. This time it was pulled at 4:16 in the morning by an 18 year old man named William Schmidt. He would be tried and found guilty of pulling the false alarm but would only receive probation. Firefighters all over the city were incensed over the punishment and I think if any of the members from Engine 54 ever see William Schmidt on the street, he may never be seen again. Last year, there were over 5,000 false alarms pulled in Baltimore City, a huge waste of time and money and sometimes, tragically, life. I think all the boxes should be removed as soon as possible. Just about everybody has a phone that could be used to call the Fire Department. When the cost of false alarms outweighs the cost of taking them out, then you will see it happen. It's always about the money.

On June 6th, D-day for those historians among us, a powerful explosion rocked the neighborhood around Engine 13. The blast occurred at 11:30 at night and everyone at Engine 13 and Truck 4 knew they would be going somewhere, they just didn't know where. A minute later they were on their way to Laurens Street and Pennsylvania Avenue for an explosion in a subway that was under construction. The blast leveled three buildings and blew out windows all up and down Pennsylvania Avenue including the Lafayette Market, which sits across the street from the subway station. Miraculously, no one was killed. The workers in the tunnel smelled gas and had run out of the tunnel before it blew. There was not even much fire, just smoldering ruins to pour water on for hours, but the fire could not be completely extinguished until the gas could be shut off. The fire was considered under control at 3:30 in the morning but A-shift remained on the scene until we relieved them at 7 a.m. It could have been a lot worse if it had happened during the day when there are people shopping on the Avenue. It was the second incident at the subway construction site recently. Last week, one of the workers was electrocuted and died in the tunnel.

It was around this time that an incident happened that was as scary as any I had encountered since I had been in the department. It was a warm day and we were glad of that because we were using another second line engine that required us to ride on the back step. Doug was driving and Mitch Johnson was in charge while Stan Williams and I rode on the back step. Holding onto the railing and letting your knees take the jolt as we hit the numerous potholes was enough to make your kidneys start complaining but that was the least of our worries. We were an inviting target for rocks and bottles as we stood out in the open and we were always on the alert for an arm cocked to throw. We were lucky that we had a Plexiglas shield that covered the top and about three feet on either side of us.

On this particular day, we were responding down Pennsylvania Avenue on our way to a report of a dwelling fire near Engine 38. As we crossed Martin Luther King (MLK) Boulevard, I heard Engine 38 say that they would handle the incident and I relaxed and looked to my right at Stan to see if he had heard it too. At that moment I saw two boys cocking their arms and I hollered to Stan to watch out. We turned our heads as two large rocks bounced off the Plexiglas shield and fell to the street. I was relieved that they had missed but Stan was enraged and reached up and gave one long push on the button to alert the guys up front to stop immediately. Doug and Mitch had no idea what had transpired but one beep meant stop and that's what Doug did. Before I could say a word, Stan was off and running but the kids had a big head start and I didn't think he could catch them. I couldn't let him go alone so I joined the chase. We had on our ¾ boots but not our turnout coats as we crossed MLK and headed for the projects. We got to 900 Argyle Ave, one of the worst high rises in the projects, and we lost sight of them but we knew what they were wearing.

We walked around front of the building and there must have been 50 people sitting on the walls and steps and in among them were our rock throwers. We walked up and grabbed each one by the arm and started to take them to the bullet proof guard shack in the hallway of the building. This was not the smartest thing to do but Stan was still fuming and I don't think he cared at the moment about what could happen to two white guys in the projects with no police around. We were immediately surrounded as we walked into the high rise at 900 Argyle Avenue and were asked what the hell we thought we were doing. I told them what had happened and that we were going to call the cops and have the kids arrested. In the guard shack was a large black woman and

I knocked on the door and told her to buzz us in. She backed up and shook her head no as the crowd swelled around us. I told her again to let us in but she continued to shake her head and now the crowd was really getting angry. I started to kick at the door with my steel toed boots as hard as I could which made a hell of a racket but didn't get us any closer to gaining entry. I guess the guard got nervous because she hit the buzzer and Stan and I with the kids in tow rushed inside and closed the door before anybody else could get in. I was really mad now and I grabbed the guard by the throat and threw her against the wall, which really set the crowd off. They started to bang on the doors and screamed at us that they were going to kill us when they got in.

Meanwhile, Doug and Mitch were frantically riding around looking for us, as they had no idea where we had gone. Back in the booth, I picked up the phone and called fire department dispatch and told them who we were and where we were and that we needed the police right away. By now, Stan had become very quiet and I was worried about what he would do next but I was pretty confident that he was not going to open the door. The people on the other side of the door were now working themselves into a frenzy, pounding on the Plexiglas door trying to get to us, but the door was not moving. Now, the mother of one of the kids appeared at the door and demanded to be let in. I told her to get everybody away from the door and I would let her in. After this was done, I buzzed her in and she started to yell at me right away but I was in no mood for this now and I started to yell back. I told her that her kid had thrown rocks at us while we were responding and I was not going to let them go no matter what she said. She accused me of calling her son a nigger, which I had not done, and said she would sue me. I then kicked her out and wondered where the cops were. It had been a good five minutes since I called, even though it seemed more like an hour. I called again and told them we were in real trouble down here and needed the cops right away. Communications told me that a cop had been beaten up on Pennsylvania Avenue and they would get there as soon as they could.

A few minutes later I could see a row of blue lights coming our way and I was able to breathe again. The cops came in force and bullied their way past the crowd and escorted us out. I was never so glad to see the cops in my life. When we got back to quarters, I had to make out an incident report and tell exactly what had happened and also explain it to the police officer that was handling the case. The next week the officer came in to see me and said, "Well, you're lucky, I talked the mother out of pressing charges against you guys." I was pissed and told him so but he said it was out of his hands, that the decision had come from higher up. He said he told the mother that we were going to a fire and had to stop because of her son. He said he didn't know the outcome of our response but that if someone had died in the fire, he would charge her son with murder. Of course, this was all bull shit but it was all he could come up with and she was gullible enough to believe it.

So it all came to a close with nothing happening to the kids for throwing rocks at firefighters while they hung on the back step of a moving fire engine.

It's enough to almost make me transfer out and it was enough for Stan. He transferred to a slower company, Truck 26 on Bowleys Lane, and I didn't blame him. Sometimes it seems as if the inmates are running the asylum and there is nothing we can do about it.

The fires never stop. There may be a lull for a few days but this is always followed by a rash of fires for one of the shifts or all of the shifts. This time it was B-shift that was catching the most fires. On August 14th, a dwelling fire that was intentionally set killed an 82-year-old man and injured three others. It was in the 1400 block of Mosher Street, a couple of short blocks from Truck 10. It was a three-story row house and the fire was on the second floor. A 90 year old woman was forced to jump from the third floor just as firefighters arrived. She sustained broken bones but was expected to live. Two other people had some serious burns but they also would survive. We later learned that earlier in the evening there was a fight outside the fire building and it was thought that one of the people involved had set the fire. The poor old man on the third floor, who hadn't been involved in the fight, was found dead and I'm sure the person that set the fire could have cared less. Life does not seem to mean much in West Baltimore.

On November 28th, a ten alarm fire destroyed a large building on President Street in Fells Point. I was off that night and I was in one of the bars in Fells Point when I heard the sirens. I didn't think too much of it until I kept hearing them and hearing them, so I walked three blocks and watched the fire on this bitter cold night. The flames were 100 feet in the air and it was a surround and drown right from the start. I walked to Duda's, the closest bar, got a few beers to go and gave them to some of the guys I knew at the fire. I know they would have done the same for me. It looked like an all-nighter and I felt for them, it was really cold. I wished them luck and walked back to the bar for a beer. When I left to go home they were still there, pouring water on the flames and freezing. It was a good night to be off.

On December 23rd, fire claimed another victim on Mosher Street, this time in the 1500 block. We were crawling down the hallway when I heard a firefighter yell that he had somebody in the bathroom. I helped two other firefighters carry the guy out to the street and he was alive but not breathing very well. He died later that night at the hospital. He was the fifth person to die in a fire in the last week. Just days before this fire, a 16 year old, a 7 year old and a 4 year old had died in a dwelling on Fairmount Avenue in West Baltimore. Also, an East Baltimore man had burned to death while smoking in bed on Saturday. It does not feel much like Christmas around here.

On New Year's Eve, we were working night work and it was early in the evening when a dwelling fire was reported in the 600 block of North Carey Street. We turned out quickly and headed west, towards Engine 8 and Truck 10's quarters. Engine 8 would be first in and we would be taking the rear. As we got closer, communications informed us that there was a report of children trapped in the house. Lt. McKinnon turned around to tell us this and we all started to pull on our air bottles. It did not sound good. We dropped our lead-off line and took the rear of the dwelling. The flames were leaping out the back windows on the second floor as we made our way up the fire escape. I was on the pipe and we dragged the 1½ inch line up the fire escape to the window. Lt. McKinnon and I moved off to the side of the window to avoid the flames as we took our helmets off to don our face pieces. I got mine on but as the Lieutenant was about to put his helmet back on, the windows on the third floor blew out and glass came raining down on us. I heard him grunt as he reached up to his head and ran his hand over his hair. "Are you ok?" I asked him. "I'll be alright," he replied and we started into the back bedroom knocking the flames down as we went.

We put the back room out and entered the hallway where we ran into Engine 8 crawling on the floor. They had put the front room out and were looking for more fire. The smoke was starting to lift and I had a chance to see if Lt. McKinnon was injured. "Do you normally have blood running down your head like that?" I said. "Oh man, I thought I got cut when that window blew." We walked down the steps and out the front door to look for an ambo but we were greeted by a scene that looked like it came right out of a movie.

While we were inside on the second floor, Truck 10 and Truck 13 had been rescuing unconscious kids from everywhere in the house. The kids had been brought outside and everywhere you looked firefighters were giving mouth to mouth and closed chest massage. Kids were on the hoods of cars and lying in the street with firefighters working feverously to save their lives. We forgot about his head as we went to see if we could help. Ambos were coming from all over town and firefighters were jumping in the ambulances with kids in their arms, still breathing into their little mouths, trying to coax some life back into them. Two girls, 4 and 5 years old were pronounced dead on arrival at University Hospital. But due to the efforts of the firefighters on the scene, five more children and two adults were alive. It was a tremendous job by everybody but especially by the truck companies. All the companies on the scene were given unit citations for their work and Lt. McKinnon was also given three stitches to close the cut on his head. We were some tired puppies when we got back to quarters and the rest of the night was relatively quiet. We enjoyed the chance to get some rest.

It has been over a year since I have ridden the ambo because a new rule was put in that you had to be an emergency medical technician to ride. I have not missed it one little bit but my joy is short lived; the city has put firefighters back on the ambo as drivers only and my turn is today. It's Feb. 26th, and it is really cold. That's not all bad though, it keeps the people off the streets somewhat. It's late in the day and we are on Mosher Street near McCulloh heading back to the station when we see smoke blowing out the back of a dwelling on McCulloh Street. It looks like an occupied dwelling and the fire looks like it is on the first floor.

We call it in and I run into the basement to make sure there is no one still inside. I don't find anyone so I make my way up to the first floor and holler but

"You would see it that way," she said in a sarcastic tone. "I'm not really sure why you're here, but you—"

"I saw you come down the hall. I was on my way up to see you." Evan eyed her purse. "Are you on your way out?"

Hannah started toward the door. "Yes, as a matter of fact."

"May I join you, then?" He stepped in front of her and took her hands before she could stop him. "There's so much I need to say to you. I'm sure you could do better for company than me, but if you'll humor me for just a little while, I'd like to clear up things I've been meaning to say to you since the night Nathanson came back from the dead."

Hannah hesitated at first, but eventually she conceded. A couple of minutes later, she and Evan were entering the Moonbeam Café. They were the only ones there, aside from the clerks, and they both decided to have coffee, in spite of the late hour. Hannah knew she wouldn't sleep much anyway, and she pulled out her credit card, insisting on paying the tab even though Evan had already beaten her to the punch. Evan won the battle in the end, and she wandered away in defeat, selecting a table that was near the back and would hopefully hide, should any other patrons happen to stroll in, what was sure to be the juiciest conversation in all of Westchester County tonight.

"Drinking it black?" When Hannah nodded, Evan sat across from her. "Me, too. Hannah, I'm glad you agreed to talk with me. I've been so worried about you since the night of the abduction—"

"You know that the doctor gave me a clean bill of health."

"Yes, he did," Evan conceded, "but I can't imagine you almost getting hypothermia is the only thing that's affected you in all of this. Hannah, you were abducted and almost murdered by your father's killer. No one would have blamed you if you'd killed him, and in fact, I came very close to doing it myself. Thankfully the police have obtained enough evidence to convince them that neither you nor I pulled the trigger and that a mystery shooter beat us to the punch. I'm almost sorry it happened that way, and even sorrier that I ever could have doubted you. Hannah, this was all my—"

"Evan." She put down her cup. "The past is behind us. You did what you felt you thought was best, and I respect your decision. In fact, I'm grateful to you for it. As much as you resented my father for what he did to you, deep down, you knew something was wrong with Augustus Nathanson and you did what you felt you had to, to protect me."

"I would do anything to protect you," Evan said after a moment. "If only you knew how much I…." He reached for her hands. "Hannah, I…I don't know how to begin to tell you how very sorry I am for all of the things I did to you, for fighting a severely misguided battle for control of your father's theater, for never owning up to the feelings I told myself I didn't have. I'm sorry about the play, about involving Dani, Alicia, Cassidy—"

"Evan." The eyes which had learned to cry again filled with tears. "I would be lying if I told you that I haven't harbored feelings for you all these years. You opened my heart the day you walked through the theater doors. I've dreamed about this, I've wanted it for more than half my life, but I know that I can't have it."

"But why? Dammit, why the hell can't you?" Evan demanded, seeming oblivious to, and completely uncaring of the fact that he'd raised his voice. "Hannah, I made the biggest mistake of my life by not believing in you. I allowed Augustus to play upon my worst fears, just as I allowed my father to play upon them when I was a boy. It's because of him that I ran scared from my own life. I need to stop running—both of us need to do that. Hannah, I understand I'm asking a lot—everything in fact—but, my darling, why won't you give us a chance?"

"Because I can't trust you. I can't trust anyone." Hannah wiped away her tears as she rose. "You've said everything I've ever wanted to hear. But I stopped believing in fantasies a long time ago because that's all they ever were—fantasies."

"Hannah…Hannah, I thought—"

"I need time," Hannah said, picking up her purse, her coffee cup, and keys. "I need to figure things out, decide what I'm going to do next. I'm not exactly sure what that will be, but whatever my next move, I need to make sure I get it right."

Evan trailed after her as she walked to the door. Putting his arm out before she could leave, he said in a broken voice, "I was rather hoping we could do that together."

"So was I," Hannah replied, "but an apology just isn't enough this time. I forgive you, Evan, and I will always care about you. But I can't give you what you want. I wish I could, and that everything could be different somehow. Despite what either of us might want, a happy ending stopped being in the cards for the two of us a lifetime ago." She offered a half smile, and then, mustering every ounce of strength possible, she walked out of the café, not looking back.

* * * *

"Ms. Rabourn, you have a visitor." Claire's cheerful voice emanated from Hannah's speaker phone. "It's your cousin Alicia."

Moving around a room that seemed so much brighter than usual with music playing in the background and sunlight streaking in through every window, Hannah thought, things were certainly panning out differently than a typical Monday back in the office did. Finding the change refreshing, she said, "Send her in."

Hannah patted her collarbone, which felt bare without her locket, something she now knew hadn't belonged to her mother but to Catherine Madenford. Crazy as it was, she still wanted the last thing her father had given her. Maybe it was just as well that the police hadn't recovered the locket and that even after venturing back down to the tunnel herself, she still hadn't been able to find it.

She closed her laptop and looked up, half expecting her cousin to come at her with a mallet. But instead, Alicia came toward her and threw her arms around her in much the same way she had Nick the night of the abduction.

"Not exactly the greeting I was expecting," Hannah remarked when they pulled apart. "Though I have to say I am relieved to know you aren't here to finish the job Augustus Nathanson didn't."

Alicia wiped her eyes. "God knows you make me crazier than crazy, Hannah. But I was worried out of my mind about you the other night, and if Evan hadn't stopped Augustus, I don't know what I would have done."

"Alicia, I—"

"Let me finish. There isn't anything in the world that I hate more than being lied to. But I know the reason you and Nick kept quiet about your involvement is because you didn't want to hurt me. That is the truth, isn't it? That even though you act as if you don't need anyone, you hurt, you feel, and you love just as much as the rest of us do. Maybe more."

"Well, I wouldn't go that far," Hannah said, floored by what was probably the most flattering assessment anyone had ever given her. "But if this is your way of saying that you forgive me, I can hug it out with the best of them."

As Alicia put her arms around her for the second time, Hannah considered that maybe her cousin was right about what she'd said. She'd endured a lifetime of hurt, and as the monster who'd murdered her father had said himself, all she'd ever wanted was to be loved. Alicia loved her. Hannah would even go so far as to say that her father had loved her, too, in his own peculiar way. But Augustus had been wrong. Her father wasn't the person she'd wanted to love her the most.

"There's something you should know, and I want you to hear it from me before you hear it from anyone else." Taking a deep breath, Hannah said, "Evan thinks I have feelings for Nick. And before you go losing it on me again, you need to understand that I only let him think that's true because—"

"You don't want him to suspect the real truth?" Alicia cocked a brow. "That as much as you want to deny it, the person that you really have feelings for, that you're in love with, is Evan?"

Glad to know that Alicia understood there was nothing between her and Nick but disturbed that she obviously knew the deeper truth, Hannah opened her mouth, about to try to set the record straight when the ringing of her phone stopped her midbreath.

"I'm so sorry to interrupt you, Ms. Rabourn," Claire said into the speaker, "but Mr. Crowley's on the phone and he's insisting that he speak with you right away."

Hannah was about to tell Claire to patch him through, but instead, she hesitated, sat back, and tapped her fingernails against her desk. The corner of her mouth lifting as she glanced at a very puzzled Alicia, she said, "Please explain to Mr. Crowley that I'm in a very important meeting and can't be disturbed. If he gives you a hard time, you have my permission, and encouragement, to go ahead and hang the phone up."

"Hang up the phone? But Ms. Rabourn, I—"

"Hannah. I want you to call me Hannah from now on. That won't be a problem for you, will it?" Hannah smiled.

"Not at all Ms. Ra—Hannah." Claire sounded dumbfounded. But her voice revealed that she, too, was wearing a big smile as she assured Hannah that her instructions would be carried out to the letter and proceeded to hang up the phone.

"Well, that was an unexpected surprise, you telling your assistant of six years that she can call you by your first name." There was a note of humor in Alicia's voice. "Where were we? Oh, yes. Evan—"

"Won't be in my life much longer. Though I am leaving him with a hell of a parting gift." Hannah handed Alicia the stack of papers that was lying beside her computer. "Augustus attempted to pay off my lawyer to make it look as though I handed my portion of the theater to Sebastian. Seeing as how he got nowhere with that, it wasn't especially difficult to make the damage he did go away. Except, I don't plan on getting too comfortable."

"You're selling your shares. To Evan, of all people—Hannah, is this some sort of joke?"

"I'm afraid not. I'm not exactly sure what I'm going to do with my life, but I've realized in these last few months that my future isn't here. I've had a sort of epiphany, like the one you had when you realized you had aspirations that went beyond the stage. I'm sure I don't need to remind you that I supported your decision to leave Rabourn Theater even though I was very much against it."

"You did," Alicia conceded. "But that was entirely different. Theater isn't my passion, or at least it isn't my greatest passion. It's yours, Hannah. It's been running through your veins since before you could talk. Or so my mother says. I realize that you don't need the money, but what exactly are you going to do with yourself with no career, retired at thirty-eight years old?"

Hannah had considered a number of possibilities and wasn't really happy with any of them. "Maybe I could help out at that stable of yours. You'd offer me a position, wouldn't you?"

"Hannah, you know I would. But I just can't imagine that everything is settled for you at Rabourn Theater, that you've done all you're meant to do here, all of the things you need and want to do."

"And I intend to rectify that." Eyeing her father's picture, which rested atop her desk and which she was seriously thinking of replacing with a potted plant, Hannah explained, "My understudy will be taking my part in the show after I leave. But I have every intention of starring in the play on opening night. This way I can live out the fantasy and finally have closure. And I'm going to do that by proving to my father that he was wrong about me, that I'm as talented as any actress that's ever performed on his stage and that his refusing to cast me was an even bigger mistake than partnering with Augustus Nathanson."

After a fair amount of persuading, Alicia appeared to have conceded. She said she was thrilled Hannah would be starring in the show on opening night, and she promised she and Nick would be there, sixth row center, cheering her on. But despite the fact that she had made up her mind, and that she'd just dodged yet another bullet, Hannah was feeling completely lost at the thought of no longer having Rabourn Theater. And she wondered whether she would ever feel whole again, living a life that Evan was no longer a part of.

* * * *

Evan sat at his desk, unable to move. He'd just hung up with his lawyer, who had given him such surprising news that he had yet to close his mouth. Following the opening night of *Ribbons and Rainbows*, Hannah was leaving Rabourn Theater. She was getting out of the theater business, and she was selling her shares exclusively to him.

When he'd regained his mobility, Evan paced the length of his office, feeling as though he was in a fog he couldn't bring himself out of. Hannah had just given him what he'd been fighting for, for half his life, what he had sacrificed everything for, and would have, at one time, killed for. But holding it in his hands didn't give him the sense of victory he'd always believed it would. Rather, it made him feel like the worst man who had ever existed, as well as the greatest fool. He didn't have to analyze the situation very hard to realize why that was.

For as long as he'd known her, Evan had always been afraid of what he felt for Hannah. He'd had his share of women, but none of them had ever made him feel what he feared more than anything—namely, that he wasn't the one in control. As a boy in Oxfordshire, he'd had no control whatsoever, and so when he'd grown up, he'd been intent on assuming control of anything he could get his hands on. He'd needed to feel powerful, and Hannah was a threat to that power. In fact, she was the greatest threat to it. And so he'd pushed her away, not only to protect her but also because he was a coward, more afraid of what he might be feeling for her than anything else.

Hannah had told him that she couldn't trust him. And Evan understood why she felt that way. In his heart, he'd told himself how he felt about her a thousand times over. But as long as he lived, he wasn't sure he would ever be able to admit his greatest truth out loud.

"It's about bloody time," he snapped, removing all traces of melancholy from his face as Chris strolled through his door. "I know you've been busy these last few weeks, but now that we know Mr. Sutherland's connection to Nathanson is no longer of importance, I need you to start focusing on more important matters. Of course, the police arrested young Ryder on the scene the day of Hannah's abduction, but Sebastian has gone off the grid. I want you to find him. And while you're at it, I want you to get a hold of Nathanson's coroner's report. I believe Sebastian is our mystery shooter, and despite the fact that neither Hannah nor I are being tried for his murder, I want to see for myself that Nathanson is really good and dead this time."

Chris was staring out the window and his eyes were bloodshot, as though he hadn't slept in a week. He was pale and his disposition appeared to be a cross between distraught and seething. Having gotten a better look at him, Evan wasn't sure he'd seen Chris looking quite so bent out of shape since the day his wife died.

He asked, "What's wrong?"

"Evelyn was having an affair."

Certain he couldn't have heard what he believed he had, Evan said, "I beg your pardon?"

"She cried herself to sleep every night after we lost the baby. She wouldn't let me hold her or touch her when she was…." Chris turned around. "Evelyn acted like she was broken, like it hurt her to be with me, and all the while she was being comforted by another man, giving herself to that man!"

"That was…years ago," Evan reasoned. "And up until now, you've heard nothing about it. Are you sure whatever source provided you with this information has any idea of what they're talking about?"

"I heard them!" Chris shouted. "The affair happened in our bed! I convinced myself I was hearing things, that I was drunk out of my mind and crashing on the couch because I was giving Evelyn her space. I sure gave her space, didn't I? My own wife turned to someone else, *spread her legs* for Oakley Sutherland!"

"Sutherland," Evan muttered, having surmised as much but attempting to make it sound as though the idea was just now occurring to him.

"The police never found Evelyn's killer. They were convinced the person driving the car that hit her was just some random speeder, but in all the years that have passed since then, I've never thought it added up."

"And you believe"—Evan lifted his eyebrows—"that the man who was her lover may have also been her killer. Or perhaps you believe that man paid someone to do his dirty work, something we both know would be just another day in the park for him."

"Sutherland isn't a man who lets things go without a fight. If he surmised Evelyn wasn't going to leave me, if she tried to end the affair and that wasn't what he wanted, he might have done something desperate. My God, man, am I crazy? Or do you think I'm dead-on?"

"What I think, " Evan said, having recently become aware that nothing was necessarily as it appeared when it came to murder, "is that you need to put everything else in your life aside and dedicate your full attention to figuring that out."

"What about my position?" Chris asked after a moment. "I know that there are plenty of people who could fill in for me at the theater but what about your personal affairs? I know there are only so many people you want involved—"

"And I stand by that notion. But I've leaned on you for too long, expected you to be at my constant beck and call. I've asked a great deal of you. I'm exceedingly grateful, but for the indefinite future, I think the people you need to be looking out for are your daughter, and yourself."

"I'll be back before you know I'm gone," Chris said as they slapped each other on the back and shook hands. "For what it's worth, I'm sure that in my absence, Hannah Rabourn will more than make up for the void."

"If only it were that simple. I'm positive I've destroyed any good feelings Hannah may have had for me, and what's worse is that in recent weeks I've managed to hurt her more than I ever have. I'm certain Hannah blames me for her father's murder, and to be perfectly honest, she isn't entirely wrong in doing so. I was with Augustus moments before it happened. Knowing how vindictive that man was, I ought to have realized what he was planning and found some way to put a stop to it. I didn't see the truth because I didn't want to see it." Collapsing into his chair, Evan said, "It doesn't surprise me that Hannah would prefer a man like Nick Lancaster. Say what you will about her, but she's a woman who sees me for who I really am."

An e-mail from his lawyer appeared on the screen of Evan's computer. He opened it and found details about the sale of Hannah's shares. Turning the screen toward Chris, he expected to see the younger man's eyes bulge. Instead, Chris merely shook his head.

"Forgive me for saying so"—Chris sat on Evan's desk—"but that's a load of crap. Yeah, you heard me. Hannah wants her little cousin's fiancé about as much as I want Bertha Walters, the old lady who designs our costumes. Hannah does see you for who you are. For some crazy reason, she actually loves you in spite of it. The question is, are you going to step up? Because if you plan on spending the next two weeks wallowing in self-pity and Hannah really does leave after opening night like everyone says she will, you may be wasting the last opportunity you're ever going to get with her."

Even had had a lifetime of opportunities. And he had blown one after the other, so afraid of his own shadow that he'd allowed the best thing that had ever happened to him to slip right through his fingers. He'd believed he was out of chances, but the truth was that Hannah hadn't gone anywhere and she wouldn't, at least not until after opening night. It seemed impossible, but if there was anyone at that theater who was even more stubborn than she was, it was him.

Evan explained the plan taking shape in his mind to Chris, assuring him that it was beyond time he took the advice of the wisest man he knew and that he planned on seizing his final opportunity with everything he had. Knowing there wasn't a doubt in his mind that he would do just that, he only prayed Hannah would accept what he had to offer.

Chapter 28

"Are you ready, Blair? Your audience is waiting for you."

Hannah turned in her chair, and the tech assisting her with her makeup stepped back as Alicia approached her. Fluttering her eyelashes—which looked about twice their actual length—she said, "They'll have to hold on for a bit. But I don't plan on making them wait long."

As Vanessa added the finishing touches to her face, Hannah reviewed the speech she would be giving after the play, announcing to the audience, cast, and crew that she would be leaving Rabourn Theater. Her time there had come to an end, but the theater's time-honored traditions had not, and the man who'd made them possible would live on inside the theater's walls for as long as they remained standing.

Hannah finally had closure about her father's death. He may not have been the man she'd wanted to believe, but she would always love him, and she knew, deep down, that her father had always loved her, too. His killer was dead, her attacker's accomplice awaiting trial, and the man in the middle of all of it had disappeared without a trace. Hannah imagined Sebastian would pop up again at some point. She only prayed, when he did, that the police would arrest him and throw away the key.

She and Nick were finally getting along. Hannah would almost go so far as to call the man her friend—they'd almost died together, and in their darkest moment, they'd given one another encouragement and strength. Nick's father was no prize, but her own had been worse, and Hannah had come to realize that neither she, nor Nick, were a product of their parents' mistakes. In truth, they had both fought to come into their own, and she was thrilled for Alicia, knowing that in just a few days she was going to be marrying the man of her dreams.

Hannah almost wished that in some alternate universe the same thing could be happening to her. But she was done wasting her time with senseless wishes. After tonight she would no longer have to think about them anymore, either.

"Break a leg!" she called to the other actresses who were standing around.

Alicia went to find her seat, and Hannah entered the backstage area to find Chris Gordon wishing everyone well. After he headed up to the sound booth to prepare to call cues, Hannah took a breath, lifted the end of her heavy skirt, and assumed her position at the front of the stage.

Hannah sang the first number, which included a dance involving several members of the chorus line. When the routine was finished, she went backstage for a quick reprieve and a costume change before coming back to sing her first duet with Evan. For as much as the scene would allow her to, Hannah tried not to look at her costar. But her attempt was unsuccessful. As Evan approached her from across the stage, she became breathless—he was as handsome as he'd been the first time she'd seen him. Evan was poised and charismatic, his voice alluring and powerful, but what was even more powerful was the man himself and the effect he had on her as he sang the words her father had written so long ago. As Evan drew her against him and pressed his warm lips against hers, Hannah realized that what she felt for him would never disappear, no matter how far apart they were. She would forever be a prisoner of her own desires.

The intermission finally came, and Hannah practically ran from the stage. She spent several more minutes in the dressing room than necessary, taking as much time for herself as she possibly could and half debating whether she wanted to do the second act of the play at all. There'd be more kissing, more touching, and more of those lyrics that cut her to the core. But in the end, Hannah realized the only person she'd be hurting by not finishing the play would be herself. And so she joined the other actors, preparing herself as best as she could for what was yet to come.

The next several numbers all went smoothly, and Hannah did what she had to, playing the part of the smitten Blair Copeland and keeping her real heart locked inside her chest. She was grateful she and Evan had not had a great amount of interaction thus far, but they were coming up on a number of scenes in which the two of them would be in very close proximity. What had her stomach in knots, though, was not the thought of the proximity itself, but the fact that Fin would tell Blair that as bewitched by her as he'd become he didn't want to see her anymore.

"Oh my sweet temptress," Evan was saying. "How badly I long to taste the nectar of your skin, to feel your body pressing against mine, your silken hair spilled against the softness of your shoulders."

"I need you, too," Hannah replied, the words catching in her throat as Evan drew her against him and began to take down her hair. As the last of the pins fell free, she shut her eyes tightly and said, "But more than that, I need to know, need to know—"

"How I feel about you?" Evan replied before she could get the rest of her line out. Smirking as he looked from her to the audience and back again, he continued, "That's a complicated question. But the answer is simple and long overdue and"—he looked into her eyes—"I intend to give it to you right here, right now."

Aware that her costar had taken a tremendous detour from the script and wondering what in the world he was up to, Hannah whispered sharply, "What the hell—?"

Evan held a finger to her lips. "I've been in love with you—rather"—he spoke up so that the audience could hear—"I have been *madly* in love with you since the moment we met."

There were quite a few gasps, but Evan continued over them. "I was a fool when I was younger, even more so of late. But I'll be damned if I'm going to allow my selfishness and my stupidity to cost me the greatest thing that's ever walked into my life. You are my heart and soul. And if you can find it in your heart to forgive me for the things I've done, then I swear to you, my darling, I am going to spend the rest of my life cherishing you the way that you deserve to be cherished."

Hannah's throat was dry, and when she tried to speak whatever she'd intended to say refused to come out. Looking at the audience, which included over five hundred people and spotting Alicia and Nick in the sixth row staring at her and Evan as though their eyes were about to pop out of their heads, she turned back to him and said, "Bravo, *Fin*. You've managed to take the art of deception to a level I wasn't even aware existed. I honestly didn't believe you could lie with such strong conviction, but apparently, I was wrong. You don't love me. You've made it abundantly clear what the true love of your life is, and what it's not."

Stepping in front of her before she could walk off the stage Evan said, "For argument's sake, let's assume you believe the true love of my life to be Rabourn Theater. I assure you that as much as I love the theater, it could never compare to my love for you. You are my missing half, Hannah. I need you more than life itself."

"You talk a good game"—Hannah blinked her blurring eyes—"but you're forgetting that I know you better than anyone. You play a convincing role on the stage, but as far as actually loving someone is concerned, I'm afraid that's where your talent comes up short."

"My actions have," Evan corrected, snapping his fingers so the stagehands who were standing nearby would prevent her from leaving. "But my feelings for you have always been exactly what they are. I knew from the moment I first saw you that you were the one woman that I could never resist. I was a fool and a coward, and I allowed my aspirations as well as my appetite for revenge to destroy the greatest gift I have ever been given. I'm abundantly aware that I've hurt you, and I'm asking you to look into your heart, your heart which is purer and warmer than any other I know, to find some way to let me in again."

"Evan," Hannah said, his words hitting her so hard she sounded out of breath, "I thought I could let myself go there with you again. But this thing between you and I is a fantasy, and that's all it ever was. It was very clever of you to take the liberty of rewriting our script, but it was also wildly inappropriate, and though I intend to refund our audience in full for today's performance, I think it's safe to say that we've given everyone enough of a show."

"No, I don't believe we have," Evan said as everyone laughed, taking hold of her hand before she could walk away. He spun her around to face him and captured her mouth with his, kissing her fully and deeply, in a manner that, in spite of her best efforts, sent a blast of heat and desire rushing through her body.

A number of gasps came from the audience but most sounded intrigued, as though they were witnessing what was possibly the most exciting show they'd ever seen. Hannah barely heard them. The softness of Evan's lips was like a drug she could never get enough of. But she forced herself to break free of her trance and placed her hands against Evan's chest, pushing him away.

"I sincerely hope you enjoyed that," she hissed, "because that was the last time you're ever going to touch me. Guard!" she exclaimed, motioning to the security personnel who were standing backstage.

"You can go ahead and run," Evan called after her as she hurried toward the exit. "But I can run as fast as you can, and I'm equally persistent. Then again, you must know that, seeing as how, as you just said yourself, you know me better than anyone."

The words tore through her, and as Hannah looked around the room at the sea of faces, all of which were staring at her, she was stopped dead in her tracks. She tore off her microphone and tossed it onto the stage. "What the hell do you want from me, Evan?"

Evan shut off his microphone in turn. “There are a lot of things I want from you. But the most important one, the one I won’t rest until I have, is your heart.”

“You broke my heart,” Hannah said, the words coming in a torrent she couldn’t control. “You shattered it in a thousand pieces, so there isn’t any part of it left that’s whole enough for me to give to you or to anyone.”

“I know I broke your heart. Doing so was the biggest regret of my existence, and until a day and a half ago I had no idea of how to move beyond that regret.”

“And what makes you think you can move beyond it now?”

“Because I love you,” Evan answered, his eyes assuring her that he meant what he said. “I don’t deserve you by any means, but I’ll be damned if I’m going to give you up without a fight. On God’s earth I swear to you that I will never love anyone else the way that I love you. You’re courageous and clever, determined and headstrong and when you think that no one’s watching, you are the kindest and most loving person in the world. Your capacity to love is tremendous, and I need that love as much as I need air. I beg of you, Hannah. Please, my dear, I need you to love me.”

Tears streamed down Hannah’s face and the lump in her throat threatened to cut off her breathing. She started to run again only to turn around and throw herself into Evan’s arms, drawing him against her and kissing him with all the love she had inside of her. Their mouths melded and Evan deepened the kiss, cradling the back of her head as though she was the most precious of treasures. The audience erupted in cheers louder than any Hannah had ever heard inside her father’s theater.

“Don’t cry, my love,” Evan whispered as he cupped her wet cheeks.

“I can’t help it. I’ve loved you since we were kids, but I never believed you felt the same way.”

"Don't ever doubt the way I feel about you, Hannah. I told myself that my need for revenge was greater than anything, but nothing could ever be greater than my love for you. If you'll allow me to, I intend to spend every day for the rest of our lives showing you just how much I love you."

"I love you so much," Hannah said, allowing the tears to flow where they would as she rested her head against the strength of Evan's chest—the most comforting place she knew.

"As I love you, Hannah," Evan whispered into her ear, "as I love you."

Epilogue

As Evan rolled onto his back, he instinctively placed his hand to his right and opened his eyes with a start when he realized Hannah wasn't on her side of the bed. He hadn't been sleeping long, probably only an hour, but Hannah had said she was coming to bed. Noting the indentation in her pillow, he hoped she hadn't had a nightmare, which she did occasionally, though she'd stopped dreaming about her father's murder months before. When she did wake from a nightmare, courageous as she was, he was always there to comfort her, and to reassure her that he would always be there to protect her no matter what.

Evan jolted fully awake when he heard a noise outside the room. He started to get up only to see the knob turn, and Hannah, whom he almost hadn't recognized, entered the room. She was wearing a sheer gown that barely concealed her figure and a mask adorned with gemstones and feathers. As she approached the bed, she removed the mask and set it down on the nightstand. With a sly smile on her face, she crawled her way toward him.

"My, my, my," Evan said, his lower half feeling as if it had been set ablaze. "What have we here?"

"Don't you recognize me?" Hannah purred. "I'm Elizabeth Crawford, the star of your upcoming production. I wanted to give you a preview of what I'd be wearing, Mr. Stage Director, seeing as how I've heard you have a fascination with costumes of the risqué variety."

Evan's shaking hands found their way to his seducer's almost-bare shoulders. As Hannah had noted, he had kept his position as stage director, and she had kept her position as board chairwoman. Unhappy with this, apparently, several of the members had stepped down from the board and sold their shares to the remaining members, a few of which they'd given to Hannah. Evan and Chris continued to keep a close eye on the secret society that had not fully disintegrated upon Evan's abandoning the ship. Rather, the group's remaining members had become even more determined at pushing their agenda, and they'd turned to Oakley Sutherland, whom Evan had decided to keep on at the theater in hopes of learning whatever secrets Nathanson had entrusted him with, whom his assistant was becoming more convinced by the day had been his wife's killer.

Determined not to focus on stressful matters tonight, and instead choosing to give his full attention to his bride-to-be, Evan fingered the lacy straps on Hannah's lingerie. "It certainly is an enticing piece. Of course, it isn't so much the costume but the actress beneath it that the director must get a feel for, if he's to know if a show will succeed."

"Ah," Hannah said as she straddled Evan's legs. "But you see, Mr. Director…" She kissed his bare chest "…if you unmask me, I'm afraid you may find that I don't look very much like Elizabeth Crawford but instead like your tyrannical board chairwoman."

Evan grasped Hannah's chin and kissed her fiercely before tossing her onto her back. He got on top of her, looked into her eyes, and said, "We best get this off of you immediately, then, Ms. Crawford. Because I want what lies within this costume more than anything in this world. And I love the woman you're hiding beneath it most of all."

THE END

WWW.JESSICALAURYN.COM

CPSIA information can be obtained
at www.ICGtesting.com
Printed in the USA
BVOW04s1322040917
493897BV00014BA/347/P

9 781640 105812